ALCTS
PAPERS ON LIBRARY
TECHNICAL SERVICES
& COLLECTIONS, no. 9

Managing Electronic Serials

Essays Based on the ALCTS Electronic Serials Institutes 1997–1999

PAMELA BLUH
Editor

FOR THE
Serials Section
of the Association
for Library Collections
& Technical Services

Brad Eden
Series Editor

AMERICAN LIBRARY ASSOCIATION
Chicago and London   2001

Special thanks to Sandra Heft
for her assistance and excellent suggestions
in editing segments of this work.

———————

While extensive effort has gone into ensuring the reliability of information appearing in this book, the publisher makes no warranty, express or implied, on the accuracy or reliability of the information, and does not assume and hereby disclaims any liability to any person for any loss or damage caused by errors or omissions in this publication.

Composition by the dotted i using Sabon and Optima in QuarkXPress 4.04 for the Macintosh

Printed on 50-pound white offset, a pH-neutral stock, and bound in 10-point coated cover stock by Batson Printing

The paper used in this publication meets the minimum requirements of American National Standard for Information Sciences—Permanence of Paper for Printed Library Materials, ANSI Z39.48-1992. ∞

Library of Congress Cataloging-in-Publication Data
    Managing electronic serials : essays based on the ALCTS electronic serials institutes, 1997–1999 / edited by Pamela Bluh for the Serials Section of the Association for Library Collections & Technical Services.
        p.   cm. — (ALCTS papers on library technical services and collections ; no. 9)
    Includes bibliographical references and index.
    ISBN 0-8389-3510-9 (alk. paper)
    1. Libraries—United States—Special collections—Electronic journals.
I. Bluh, Pamela. II. Association for Library Collections & Technical Services. Serials Section. III. Series.
Z692.E43 M36 2001
025.17′4—dc21   00-067646

Printed in the United States of America

05 04 03 02 01   5 4 3 2 1

CONTENTS

DISCOVERING ELECTRONIC SERIALS
An Introduction

PAMELA BLUH

Ancient mythology abounds with legends in which animate and inanimate objects are miraculously transformed and take on completely new characteristics, not just once, but often multiple times in rapid succession. This phenomenon, found in the traditions of many different cultures ranging from European to Asian, is known as shape-shifting, in which objects cast off human attributes and appearances and assume other, often animal, forms.[1] A magnificent example may be found in the Welsh legend describing the birth of the mythical poet, Taliesin. In the story, Ceridwen has prepared a potion containing three magical drops which must be stirred for a year and a day. Toward the end of that time, as Gwion Bach is stirring the cauldron, the three magic drops land on his finger, and he flees in an attempt to escape Ceridwen's wrath. Infuriated, Ceridwen follows him.

> [Gwion] changed himself into a hare. [Ceridwen] became a greyhound. He leaped into a river and became a fish, and she chased him as an otter. He became a bird and she a hawk. Then he turned himself into a grain of wheat and dropped among the other grains on a threshing-floor, and she became a black hen and swallowed him.[2]

These changes, which appear so fanciful and imaginative, were quite purposeful. Occurring in response to real or perceived threats, they served as a means to escape, frighten, or mislead predators; as a way of coping with adversity; and as a way to adapt to changes in immediate circumstances or in the broader environment.

In many respects, the changes we have come to accept, even expect, with regard to electronic serials have some of the characteristics of shape-shifting—fantastic, frightening, fabulous, and frequently mysterious.

Electronic serials seem to be in a constant state of flux, assuming new forms quickly and spontaneously, often without warning, requiring rapid response, and continually challenging us, literally and figuratively, to come to grips with them. The evolution of electronic serials, which we sometimes perceive as confusing and chaotic—perhaps because we are experiencing it firsthand rather than examining it from a more tolerant, forgiving historical perspective—may be seen, after some careful analysis and assessment, as quite deliberate.

BACKGROUND

In July 1991, the *"Directory of Electronic Journals and Newsletters* list[ed] approximately 30 electronic journal titles, over 60 newsletters, and 15 'other' titles, including items such as newsletter digests."[3] In the spring of 2000, *New Jour,* an Internet archive of online electronic journals and newsletters, listed 8,593 electronic journals.[4] Where and when will this spectacular explosion end? No single, satisfactory answer exists. Hardly a day goes by without a question being posed about some aspect of electronic serials—how to catalog them, how to manage hypertext links, how to determine which publications are worthy, how to deal with site licenses, how to handle the technical details of access and security—the list goes on and on. The questions, coupled with the seemingly endless array of new titles in electronic form, provide ample evidence that we have a long way to go before the topic becomes trite or exhausted.

In retrospect, it is clear that there has been a steady and irreversible movement toward electronic serials for nearly forty years. The computer-generated printed texts of the early 1960s may be seen as precursors of today's electronic serials and perhaps even as foreshadowing the electronic serials revolution. This was followed by the distribution of texts in an electronic form in conjunction with an identical paper product. CD-ROM products then came into vogue, but eventually were superseded as online access became increasingly desirable and feasible. For a time, the online electronic serial continued to represent primarily an electronic version of a printed publication until value-added features, such as indexing and searching, were incorporated, and, by the late 1980s, a number of electronic journals with no corresponding printed version began to appear.[5] On the library scene, the *Newsletter of Serials Pricing Issues (NSPI)* made its debut on February 27, 1989, followed in 1990 by *Public Access Computer Systems Review (PACS Review).*

Among scholarly journals, *Postmodern Culture* is frequently cited as the first true electronic journal, publishing its first issue in September 1990. During the 1990s, a new generation of electronic serials began to appear. Not only did these journals have no print counterpart, they were "packaged" with all kinds of sophisticated, embedded capabilities such as sound and hypertext links. And the rest, as they say, is history. The interesting thing about this timeline is that it is not linear, with the steps following neatly and tidily one after another. Instead, as Lancaster points out, "the actual evolution is not easy to depict since all of the steps now co-exist."[6]

Why are electronic serials still of interest to such a vast number of people? We cannot credit a single event or circumstance for this remarkable situation. Rather it appears to be the result of the intersection of a number of conditions. Throughout the 1980s, wave after wave of journal price increases triggered often wholesale subscription cancellations that left collections leaner but in the end may not have saved libraries much money. Despite these massive journal cancellation projects, collections expanded, creating concerns about space. At the same time, advances in technology were making it feasible to store larger and larger quantities of information electronically as well as to access and retrieve that information more quickly and efficiently. Users began clamoring for rapid access to more and more information, not only while in the library, but also from office or from home and eventually from anywhere, at any time. By the early 1990s, libraries began to consider electronic publications not only as a way to save money and to make better use of space, but more importantly as a means of improving accessibility to, and timely delivery of, information.

Although the growth of electronic serials continued methodically during the 1990s, one significant component of the equation was still missing. The catalyst responsible for bringing the various elements together, thus launching the meteoric rise of electronic serials, was the Internet and the amazing and virtually instantaneous dominance of the World Wide Web. By the end of the decade of the nineties, electronic serials finally seemed to offer librarians not only a viable alternative for saving money as well as space, but also an acceptable means of conducting and disseminating research. This is not to suggest that e-journals are the panacea to solve all the access, financial, and space problems facing libraries, but, rather, simply one mechanism within the arsenal of mechanisms libraries may consider for making their collections more accessible, approachable, and affordable.

BACKGROUND

This publication has had a rather long "gestational" period. The project's beginnings may be traced to a meeting of a small group of librarians during the 1996 Midwinter Meeting of the American Library Association in San Antonio, where, among other things, programming ideas for the Serials Section of ALCTS were considered. A number of suggestions surfaced, but none captured the group's imagination as completely as that of electronic serials. As a result, a program entitled "At Issue: Dimensions of Seriality in an Electronic World" was presented at ALA in the summer of 1997. The purpose of the program was twofold: to provide a broad-brush introduction to a topic that was wreaking havoc with our traditional sense of order and craved clarification and explanation; and to test the waters, so to speak, for a more ambitious institute on electronic serials.

Attendance at the program was beyond the planning committee's wildest dreams, and offered reassurance that the topic was both timely and well suited for more detailed, in-depth consideration. The first Electronic Serials Institute, "A Capital Idea: Electronic Serials from Acquisition to Access," was held in Washington, D.C., in September 1997. To satisfy the many requests for institutes in other regions of the country, a second institute, "Through the Arch: Electronic Serials from Acquisition to Access," was held in St. Louis in 1998, followed by a third, "Blazing the Trail: Electronic Serials from Acquisition to Access," in Portland, Oregon, in April 1999. The institutes were popular and well attended, and generated many inquiries concerning the availability of the presentations in a printed form. Although planners for each institute had discussed publishing the papers, the logistics and timing for such a project began to mesh only in mid-1999.

Given the ongoing and persistent interest in the subject, the notion of publishing the presentations from the three electronic serials institutes gained momentum. However, considerable time had elapsed since the first institute in 1997 and serious concerns arose that the information presented then would no longer be relevant or timely. Although timeliness is important, it became obvious that in this day and age, any publication on the topic of electronic serials was likely to be passé well before the type had been set and the ink had dried on the paper! Although changes and advances in technology continue to make the subject of electronic serials fascinating and compelling, there were legitimate concerns about preparing a publication that deals with such an intricate and elusive topic. The institutes were not comprehensive in their coverage, and this publication does not attempt to be so, either; the topic is simply too complex and diverse to be embraced successfully in its entirety. Rather, the purposes of this publication are to share some of ideas that were articulated and some of the basic concepts that were discussed at the institutes and to give readers a sense of the critical issues, the practical considerations, and the future possibilities that the topic encompasses—an overview, in a sense, of the breadth and depth of the topic.

Although the primary focus of this publication is on a selection of papers from the institutes, other aspects of the topic not covered during the institutes also deserved consideration. In order to enhance the publication and make it more balanced and well rounded, several additional contributions were solicited.

OVERVIEW OF THE CONTENTS

A number of common threads run through the chapters: that electronic serials are complex and capricious; that economic and business considerations, rather than technological issues, are paramount; and that we must seize the day, not wait for the perfect moment to get involved and not expect the perfect solution for our problems. This book will not be able to eliminate the uncertainties, the ambiguities, and the mysteries surrounding the topic, but perhaps it will help to minimize them and provide a fresh perspective on selected aspects of the topic.

Regina Reynold's paper on seriality is the perfect introduction to a discussion of electronic serials. As head of the National Serials Data Program (NSDP) at the Library of Congress, Regina writes and speaks widely on the topic of seriality, and as traditional print publications are being eclipsed by alternative publication forms, she explains why a new approach to seriality is essential. In addition to some valuable background information about the evolution of the term *seriality*, Regina's chapter will help demystify a very complicated and fluid topic and set the stage for the discussions that follow.

Ronald Larsen's fascinating chapter "Saddlepoints in Serials" is based on his keynote presentation at the first Electronic Serials Institute in Washington, D.C., in 1997. He challenges us to question the validity of several long-held assumptions about the nature of our collections, and consider whether these assumptions are outmoded and should be updated or even replaced by more relevant suppositions. Ron has been engaged in research related to digital collections and information management for a number of years, most recently at the Defense Advanced Research Projects Agency (DARPA). In mid-1999, he returned to the University of Maryland as executive director of the Maryland Applied

Information Technology Initiative (MAITI). He is uniquely qualified to speculate and hypothesize on the future of digital technology, and his chapter is both tantalizing and thought provoking.

To appreciate fully the rapid changes in the delivery of information in the past decade or so, Friedemann Weigel suggests that it is necessary to understand a little of the history of printing and scholarly research. By virtue of his position as director of Information Systems at Harrassowitz, and as a consequence of his participation in several international standards organizations, including ICEDIS (International Committee on EDI for Serials) and EDItEUR (Pan-European Book Sector EDI Group), he has been involved with the development and deployment of a variety of electronic products and services. In addition to providing a brief historical overview, Friedemann's chapter examines some of the questions librarians must consider if they intend to include electronic serials as part of the library's standard offerings.

The task of integrating electronic serials into routine operations is more complicated than simply substituting a print serial for an electronic counterpart or adding an electronic title to enhance the print collection. Sharon Cline McKay, field account executive, Western United States for SilverPlatter, was present at all three Electronic Serials Institutes, first as an attendee and later as a presenter. From her unique perspective not only as observer and participant, but also as a result of her substantial background and experience in the world of serials, she elaborates on several issues that librarians should consider before launching wholeheartedly into the electronic arena.

Although the attraction of electronic serials is very strong, the management and technical implications inherent in introducing them into the collection are often overlooked or minimized. George Machovec's chapter expands on and reemphasizes the importance of considering these aspects throughout the decision-making process. Following his practical suggestions could easily make the difference between a smooth introduction and one fraught with complications. This chapter is based on presentations George made at the second and third Electronic Serials Institutes, and is rich in information on the preparations libraries should make when introducing electronic serials.

Dan Tonkery's chapter, "Seven Common Myths about Acquiring and Accessing E-journals," takes a slightly tongue-in-cheek look at a number of our dearly held beliefs. Dan is president of the Faxon Company and has had a remarkable career in the medical and academic library communities. Based on his experiences, both in libraries and in the vendor industry, Dan is well positioned to set the record straight with regard to electronic serials by explaining the genesis of these ideas.

Many librarians are not sensitive to the complex issues surrounding the licensing of electronic resources. To help them understand this topic, Sarah Sully, an attorney with Morrison & Foerster LLP, presents "How Intellectual Property Laws Affecting Libraries Are Changing," which includes a synopsis of recent developments in copyright law. Before returning to the private practice of law, Sarah was the general counsel and director of Publisher Relations at JSTOR. Her chapter explains a number of issues surrounding copyright law, so that librarians are able to make well-informed decisions about licensing agreements for electronic products and services.

Faye Chadwell focuses her remarks directly on what librarians must do to introduce electronic resources into their collections. Faye is head of Collection Development at the University of Oregon, and "A License to Kill For . . ." is based on her presentation at the third Electronic Serials Institute in Portland in 1999. She provides a framework librarians can use to negotiate agreements, and discusses the "real-world" situation for bringing electronic serials to the user.

Having articulated some of the management, technical, and licensing issues, librarians must come to grips with a number of practical matters, including the cataloging of electronic serials. Norma Fair, Steve Shadle, and Beverley Geer have combined their considerable knowledge in a chapter entitled "Cataloging Electronic Resources: The Practicalities" to examine the current state of cataloging electronic serials. Norma is a member of the Cataloging Department at the University of Missouri, Columbia, and, with Beverley Geer, currently serials librarian for Questia Media, presented the cataloging component at the second Electronic Serials Institute in 1998. Steve is the serials cataloger at the University of Washington and presented the cataloging component at the third Electronic Serials Institute. Based on their collective experience, these three authors offer sound practical advice and provide details on the intricate nature of cataloging electronic serials.

Frequently, when the subject of electronic serials is discussed, the dialogue tends to be somewhat one-sided. In our eagerness to introduce electronic serials, we often forge ahead before we have adequately considered the public service ramifications and requirements. Raye Lynn Thomas, reference coordinator at the Ruben Salazar Library at Sonoma State University, presented a paper at the third Electronic Serials Institute entitled "Nuts and Bolts: Public Service in an Electronic Environment." Her guidelines and concrete suggestions focus attention on the variety of factors to be considered as electronic resources are contemplated and subsequently introduced. She stresses the importance of creating a collegial environment by involving staff members from several organizational areas in the decision-making process.

The Electronic Serials Institutes were designed to combine the practical with the theoretical, and this publication attempts to do the same: to give readers an overview of the major issues being addressed and, at the same time, give them a hint of the potential of this new medium. At the conclusion of each institute, there was an opportunity to recap or summarize the institute's events, but more importantly, to ponder unrestrictedly the future of electronic resources. At the third institute, Tom Leonhardt presented the synopsis, aptly entitled "Another New Frontier: Trailblazing Electronically." Tom is the director of the library at the Oregon Institute of Technology, and the metaphor he has chosen to reflect on the future of electronic serials is both entertaining and highly appropriate.

As electronic serials continue to proliferate, there seems to be a corresponding increase in the amount of information about them. "Sources and Resources" presents a selection of online and traditional references. Katharina Klemperer, director of Product Development in North America for Harrassowitz, contributes resources from the online directory "Electronic Journals: A Selected Resource Guide."[7] A list of more conventional sources was compiled by Pamela Bluh.

CONCLUSION

E-book, e-commerce, e-machine, e-serials, e-Bay—it's a "rE-volution!" The speed at which things electronic have infiltrated the marketplace and insinuated themselves into our daily lives is simultaneously frightening and exhilarating. Who would have predicted, when e-serials first materialized, that we would be so completely dominated by them? We are caught up in an evolutionary, even revolutionary, cycle that gives no evidence of subsiding. The pervasiveness and rapidity with which electronic serials have invaded our domain, combined with their elusive nature and the difficulty of capturing their essence in a substantive fashion, makes them doubly intriguing. Their changeable nature makes writing about electronic serials, and describing their attributes as well as their shortcomings, problematic and adds another dimension to the ongoing debate about the validity and authenticity of electronic information. These difficulties should not deter us from providing a perspective into the vast, ever-changing universe of electronic serials. On the contrary, they make the exercise more challenging and exciting. Like the mythological shape-shifters, electronic serials will continue to evolve, changing their characteristics to best meet the needs of librarians, publishers, and the community of readers.

NOTES

1. "A change of physical form brought about by or as if by supernatural means." *Webster's Third New International Dictionary of the English Language Unabridged* (Springfield, Mass.: Merriam-Webster, 1993), 2087; and *Man, Myth, and Magic: The Illustrated Encyclopedia of Mythology, Religion, and the Unknown*, ed. Richard Cavendish, new ed. (New York: M. Cavendish, 1997), 2354–2357.

2. T. W. Rolleston, *Celtic Myths and Legends* (London: Bracken Books, 1986), 414.

3. Linda Langschied, "Electronic Journal Forum: Column I," *Serials Review* 18, no. 1–2 (spring–summer 1992): 131.

4. See: http://gort.ucsd.edu/newjour/

5. For detailed information on the history of electronic publishing, see F. W. Lancaster, "The Evolution of Electronic Publishing," *Library Trends* 43, no. 4 (spring 1995): 518–523; and John H. Barnes, "One Giant Leap, One Small Step: Continuing the Migration to Electronic Journals," *Library Trends* 45, no. 3 (winter 1997): 404–415.

6. Lancaster, "The Evolution of Electronic Publishing," 519.

7. See: http://www.harrassowitz.de/ms/ejresguide.html

1

Seriality and the Web

REGINA ROMANO REYNOLDS

The advent of the World Wide Web in 1993 threw bibliographic control efforts into a turmoil. "Can we catalog the Web?" "Can we *not?*" "Which resources?" "How?" Libraries are still struggling with these questions. Despite the struggles caused by this revolutionary category of resource, it is to be hoped that one day serialists will recognize that a benefit of the chaos caused by Web resources was to force an overdue examination of the current division of the bibliographic universe into monographs and serials.

BACKGROUND

Although some think of serials as a materials format—what AACR2 calls a "class of materials," along with "sound recording," "computer file," or "book"—a serial is, in reality, a "type of publication" (AACR 0.25).[1] AACR2, at present, acknowledges only two types of publications: monographs and serials. To be considered a serial, a publication must be issued in successive, numbered or dated parts with the intention of being continued indefinitely. These requirements make it necessary that such obviously serial-like publications as online magazines, which are seamlessly updated rather than being divided into separate issues, be cataloged as monographs, calling into question the entire monograph-serial dichotomy.

In 1997, prompted in part by the twin forces of online publications and online catalogs, the Joint Steering Committee for AACR (JSC) held an International Conference on the Principles and Future Development of AACR in Toronto. At that conference, Jean Hirons and Crystal Graham presented a paper, "Issues Related to Seriality," which resulted in proposed revisions to AACR to accommodate seriality and which has spurred counterpart efforts to revise and similarly update two other international standards for serials: ISBD(S) and the *ISDS Manual,* which contain rules for ISSN assignments worldwide.[2]

This chapter will look at the origins of the seriality discussion in relation to the emergence of new forms of electronic publishing, summarize the current state of rule revision efforts to accommodate seriality, describe the evolution of the current rule revision proposals, and finally, note some unresolved issues and pose some questions about how seriality might be handled in the future.

ORIGINS OF THE SERIALITY PROBLEM

A serial in the digital world is conceptually not really an object or even a sequence of distinct objects—it's a *process* that is embodied in an object such as a web site, and the process aspect of continued publication of content, of being a serial, is a critically important aspect of the web site's behavior and properties that is important to capture. The network environment and changing publication practices challenge us to think again about how we define a serial.[3]

Clifford Lynch and Cecilia Preston describe a problem that serialists had recognized in the print world, but that became critical only with the arrival of serials on the World Wide Web. Before the Web, it was no secret among serials catalogers that AACR's simple division of the bibliographic universe into serials and monographs just did not work in some cases, such as loose-leafs, which some libraries catalog as serials and others as monographs. Just as there are creatures that fall somewhere between plants and animals, just as there are an infinite number of shades of grey between black and white, by the mid-1990s it had become clear that publications exist that are neither serials nor monographs, but that share some of the characteristics of each.

Almost overnight, following the arrival of the Web, challenges to the definition of a serial began to arrive at the National Serials Data Program, the ISSN center in the United States. Publishers began applying for ISSNs (International Standard Serial Numbers) for what they thought were serials. One such early application was for an online "magazine" and, as if to emphasize the dilemma this would-be serial presented, it even used the word *magazine* in its title. In fact, it was a Web site, consisting of current news and events from a particular geographic area. The "magazine" was not divided into issues—whether numbered or not—and, thus, it could not be assigned an ISSN. Even though it didn't walk exactly like a serial, it sure quacked like a serial. Nonetheless, it clearly did not meet the current definition of *serial*. Efforts to explain the ISSN refusal to the publisher were difficult. He complained loudly in words to this effect: "If it's not a serial, then what is it—surely not a book?"

Other categories of materials also come into question. Some have wondered if libraries should try to catalog discussion lists and, if so, how? Such lists certainly seemed capable of being published indefinitely. Each posting could be regarded as a "part," but such postings are usually not numbered and many postings carry the same date. Digests of lists pose another question. These digests are dated, and usually there is only one digest per day. And what about newspapers on the Web? On the one hand, how could a newspaper be anything but a serial? On the other hand, where are the numbered parts? How could an online newspaper be cataloged using existing rules?

The makeup and "behavior" of online resources also present problems. Catalogers would go to a Web site and be confronted with a host of questions: This is clearly an ongoing publication, but is it a serial? Is it one serial or several serials? Is the Web site a main series with the other ongoing components being serials within that series? Are mirror sites separate publications? Should different file formats be cataloged on different records?

The overwhelming problem was this: Suddenly the little trickle of items that did not seem to be either monographs or serials—a trickle that librarians had safely ignored for years—threatened to become a flood. Questions arose in serials cataloging departments when trusted annual reference books appeared online as continuously updated directories, or when abstracting and indexing services long cataloged as serials were published online in the form of updating, searchable databases. Did it seem logical that a publication was a serial in printed form but a monograph in online form? The time had come to reexamine the very definition of *serial*.

WHAT IS "SERIALITY"?

The word *seriality* first appeared in the 1988 revision of AACR2 along with the term *computer files*. In Rule 0.25, the 1978 edition states,

"Give the area 3 details relating to the cartographic materials before those relating to the serial."[4] In the 1988 revision, the same instruction reads, "Give details relating to the cartographic material or the computer file and those relating to its seriality. . . ."[5] Another instance of the term *seriality* in connection with the cataloging of electronic resources appears in MARBI proposal 93-4, "Changes to the USMARC Bibliographic Format (Computer Files) to Accommodate Online Information Resources," dated November 20, 1992.[6] The concept of seriality came to the forefront, however, in 1996 when Hirons and Graham presented "Issues Related to Seriality" at the JSC meeting in Toronto.[7] In their paper, they defined *seriality* as an attribute of publication and deliberately sidestepped using the term *serial* in order to focus on how to provide information that needs to be captured in a catalog record and not limit the discussion to a specific kind of publication.

As Hirons and Graham described it, *seriality* refers to the condition of being published over time and to the potential for change in every aspect that is recorded in the bibliographic description, and as Hirons and Regina Reynolds later declared in the title of their 1999 *Library Review* article, "Seriality: It's Not Just for Serials Anymore."[8] Monographs with ongoing supplements, encyclopedias issued in fascicles, many legal publications, reports of ocean expeditions, and many other kinds of publications all exhibit seriality without being serials. In fact, in no environment is seriality more in evidence than in the online environment, where one of the few predictable attributes of these resources is that they are going to continue. The widespread adoption of the term *seriality* into the bibliographic lexicon following the presentation of the Hirons and Graham paper is an indication that the concept filled a real need in the growing discussion of digital resources.

CURRENT STATE OF RULE REVISION

Following the JSC Toronto conference, Jean Hirons was asked to prepare rule revision proposals that would embody the recommendations in the Hirons and Graham paper. With the assistance of four working groups drawn from CONSER libraries and others within the U.S. and international bibliographic communities, Hirons drafted the April 1999 report, "Revising AACR2 to Accommodate Seriality."[9] After the 1999 JSC meeting, Hirons was charged with preparing rule revisions based on the recommendations that had been approved.

Revising AACR2 to accommodate seriality would be difficult enough under any circumstances, but the JSC added an additional mandate to the charge of rule revision—a requirement for compatibility with international standards. So, like Ginger Rogers, who had to do all Fred Astaire's steps backwards and in high heels, those revising AACR2 had to write many new rules while trying to "harmonize" existing serial rules and the new rule proposals with ISBD(S) and the rules for ISSN assignment, both of which were also undergoing revision to accommodate new kinds of resources.

Although much work remains to be done, significant progress has been made toward accommodating the seriality of Web resources in international cataloging rules and standards. The JSC has approved a multilevel model defining two new types of publications: "finite" and "continuing," with "continuing" being further subdivided into "serials" (defined much the same as they are now) and "integrating resources" (such as databases and Web sites). In February 2000, Hirons submitted a complete revision of Chapter 12 and revisions to other pertinent rules to the JSC. The revised Chapter 12 is entitled "Continuing Resources" and includes new rules to describe integrating resources as well as new rules for selecting the source of title and transcribing the titles of Web resources. Both the ISBD(S) working group and the working group for ISSN manual revision have also approved the new model. ISBD(S) has adopted the term "continuing resources" and has provisionally agreed that the revised standard will be called ISBD(CR): Serials and Other Continuing Resources.

The Model

The AACR type-of-publication model (fig. 1), approved by the JSC, solves the problem of how to categorize online databases, Web sites, and other ongoing resources that do not meet the current definition of *serial*. This solution has been achieved by defining a new category, "continuing resources," at the highest level of the model. Continuing resources are those that have no predetermined end, while finite resources do have such an end. Continuing resources are subdivided into serials (a relatively unchanged category) and integrating resources, the category that includes databases and Web sites. Finite resources are also divided into two categories: those that are complete, consisting of resources that are complete as issued, and those that are incomplete but continue for a predetermined period. Incomplete resources can be completed by means of successive issues or in an integrating manner. A Web site updated for the duration of a conference and then removed from the Web would be an example of a finite integrating resource.

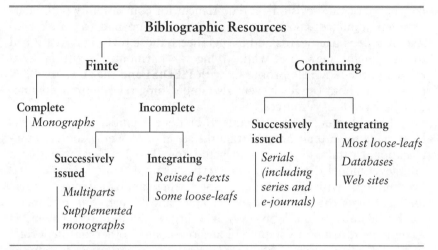

FIGURE 1   AACR Type-of-Publication Model

"Continuing resources" is an umbrella category that recognizes the seriality common to all resources that continue over time. The proposed definition of "continuing resource" is "a bibliographic resource that is issued over time, usually with no predetermined conclusion. Continuing resources include serials and integrating resources."[10] The subcategories of continuing resources are differentiated on the basis of what Hirons calls their different "forms of issuance." Serials are characterized by being issued in discrete parts that remain discrete, while integrating resources add new material seamlessly to an existing whole. The current model contains two subcategories of continuing resource: successively issued and integrating. Serials comprise the successively issued category, while databases, loose-leaf services, and Web sites comprise the category called integrating. However, the model was deliberately constructed to be able to accommodate future forms of issuance and any future categories of resources within a form of issuance that might emerge for continuing resources, especially in the realm of electronic resources. If, for example, a new form of issuance, called "conglomerating" were to become possible in the electronic environment, this new form could simply take its place as a third branch under the "continuing" umbrella, beside "successively issued" and "integrating."

Serials

The AACR2 rule revision proposals submitted in February 2000 define serials in a way that is very similar to the current definition, thus preserving this as a distinct category of material and allowing for specific rules in the cataloging code to accommodate successive issuance. However, the revised definition of *serial* is more accommodating to electronic resources. The proposed new definition reads:

> Serial. A continuing resource in any medium issued in a succession of discrete parts, usually bearing numeric or chronological designations, that usually has no predetermined conclusion. Examples of serials include journals, magazines, electronic journals, directories, annual reports, newspapers, newsletters of an event, and monographic series.[11]

Differences from the current definition include: (1) the substitution of the term *continuing resource* for *publication,* an accommodation for electronic resources; (2) the addition of the words "succession of discrete parts" to differentiate serials from integrating resources (whose parts do not remain discrete); (3) the addition of "usually" with regard to numeric or chronological designation in order to harmonize with ISSN rules; and (4) the substitution of "that usually has no predetermined conclusion" for "intended to be continued indefinitely," another accommodation that provides more flexibility for Web-based resources. The examples in the definition were also updated to make it clear that electronic journals still fall into the category of "serial."

Integrating Resources

"Integrating resources" is a category created primarily for electronic resources, because they are the most numerous kind of resource to integrate new material seamlessly into existing material, although it also includes ongoing loose-leaf publications. An integrating resource is defined as: "a bibliographic resource that is added to or changed by means of updates that do not remain discrete and are integrated into the whole. Examples include items that are loose-leaf for updating, and Web sites."[12] Creation of this category allowed separate rules to be developed to accommodate the characteristics that set integrating resources apart from traditional serials. For example, there is no requirement that integrating resources have designations (volume numbering or distinctive dates), and, therefore, transcription of a numerical or chronological designation is not required in describing these resources.

One of the most notable differences between successively issued and integrating resources is that, in the absence of ongoing archiving, a cataloger has no choice about what will form the basis of the description: The resource can be described only from the information present in the resource at the time it is cataloged. Because earlier iterations of the resource are no longer available, the bibliographic community generally felt when the title of an integrating resource changed, a separate record under the earlier title was not desirable, but, rather, all title changes should remain on one record, a practice known as "latest entry" cataloging under the pre-AACR2 rules for serials. Handling title changes in this way is one of the more notable and distinctive provisions for the cataloging of integrating resources.

New Rules for the Description of Continuing Electronic Resources

Several of the other rule revisions proposed for AACR will help accommodate the seriality of online resources. These include considering the entire source in order to select the title and giving preference to the title source that gives the most complete representation of the title. These accommodations for recording the titles of continuing electronic resources grew out of a study done by one of the AACR revision groups. The group analyzed title presentations on approximately 130 online continuing resources and concluded that no one title source is most appropriate for transcribing the title in all cases. Therefore, the proposed rules for continuing electronic resources are much more flexible than the rules for printed serials. Another of the AACR rule revisions, also accepted for the *ISSN Manual,* is aimed at solving a common problem found on Web resources: title presentations that begin with such words as "Welcome to." The proposed rule recommends that these words not be recorded in the title proper, by instructing the cataloger either to choose a source that does not include them, or, if such a source does not exist, to delete the introductory words and explain the deletion through the use of a note and an added entry.

EVOLUTION OF THE REVISION EFFORT

The solutions described here did not spring full-blown from the brows of those involved in the revision efforts, but, rather, have evolved dialectically since the Toronto conference. The involvement of the four revision groups mentioned earlier, presentations at meetings and conferences, articles, personal and electronic discussions—all contributed to the process. In dialectic fashion, theses were developed, antitheses were proposed and finally resolved and combined into what is hoped are coherent syntheses. The main areas of evolution affecting Web resources were the model, the use of latest and successive entry, and the categorization of electronic journals.

Evolution of the Model

The first question many ask about the solution to the monograph-serial dichotomy is why a third category wasn't developed, something between serials and monographs. First, those developing the models recognized that a commonality exists among all ongoing publications that must be taken into account. They all need to be described at a higher level of abstraction than a finite, complete work, and records for all need to be able to accommodate change. Furthermore, it was felt that the presence of a third category would only add to the choices catalogers had to make and would allow for more gray areas between the categories. After much discussion and deliberation, it was decided that a multi-tiered model would be more logical and would offer more flexibility to accommodate future types of publications.

The model presented earlier in this chapter differs significantly from the models proposed in the Hirons and Graham paper.[13] In that paper, two models were offered as solutions to the present monograph-serial model. Model B, which redefined *serial* by removing the requirements for numbering and for successive parts, was recommended as the short-term solution. Model C, which divided the bibliographic universe between static and ongoing publications, was offered as a longer-term solution, but one that would be problematic to implement because it would require significant changes to cataloging rules as well as to bibliographic utilities and local systems.

Problems with Model B began to surface as soon as the revision group dealing with the redefinition of *serial* began to work. Rather than eliminating the problems associated with defining a serial, the proposal seemed to add to the problems. Once the requirements for numbering and for successive parts were removed from the current definition, little was left to distinguish between monographs and serials in the online world, where intention to continue indefinitely is made explicit even less often than in the print world. Additionally, the need to distinguish between databases and loose-leafs that were intended to continue indefinitely, and those that were not, seemed needless.

Thus, "Modified Model C" was born, the model that set the basic structure for the current model.[14] The terms *static* and *ongoing* were later changed to *finite* and *continuing*. *Static* seemed to convey a stodginess unflattering to monograph publications and catalogers, while *ongoing* was felt by the international community to be difficult to translate and was replaced by *continuing*. Additionally, the model was changed to show that finite resources can include those that are incomplete when issued but do have a predetermined end. Previous versions of the model incorrectly implied that only continuing resources could be integrating, but because integrating is really a form of issuance, it can apply to any resource issued over time. It will be noted in the introduction to the revised Chapter 12 that rules for integrating resources can be applied both to finite and to continuing resources.

Latest and Successive Entry

The nature of Web resources prompted one of the most lengthy and difficult debates of the entire AACR rule revision process. This debate revolved around the question of how to handle title changes of integrating resources, especially online integrating resources. In the current Chapter 12, title changes are handled by a practice known as successive entry. According to successive entry, each time a major change in title or main entry occurs, a new record is made. Using this practice, titles can be cataloged and shelved according to the title they had at the time of publication, a practice that works reasonably well for print publications, but one many felt was not applicable to online integrating resources. When a database or Web site changes title, the old title completely disappears from the resource, thus causing many in the library cataloging community to determine that they did not want to continue to provide a record in the catalog for the title that was no longer present. Latest entry, with its use of one record for current and former titles, was felt to be better suited to the behavior of these resources. Additionally, a form of latest entry has long been used for title changes to loose-leaf publications, and because databases and Web sites are currently being cataloged as monographs, latest entry is already being applied to these publications as well.

Those in favor of using latest entry for integrating resources pointed out that the practice worked well for loose-leafs, and did not seem to be causing noticeable problems in the albeit limited experience of those cataloging databases and Web sites as monographs. Thus, many favored codifying this practice in the new rules for handling title changes to integrating resources. However, latest entry had at least one large drawback as well as several smaller ones. The most serious drawback to use of latest entry cataloging is that this form of cataloging is incompatible with current ISSN assignment and database practices. An ISSN is assigned to a key title, a standardized form of the title based on the title on the serial at the time of ISSN registration. When the key title changes in anything but a very minor way, a new ISSN is assigned. The key title is the main entry on record in the ISSN database, and there is one record per ISSN and key title. Because the ISSN is currently being assigned to databases on an experimental basis, and because the ISSN Network has provisionally endorsed the concept of continuing resources and is proposing to assign the ISSN to certain Web sites, the ISSN database would, in the future, need to be composed of records for both serials and integrating resources.

An additional drawback to latest entry records is that they can become long and cumbersome as titles, issuing bodies, publishers, and places all change, sometimes at different times. Constructing a "snapshot" of a serial at a particular point in time from a latest entry record can be difficult because the record does not always make clear which bibliographic elements apply to which time period. For this reason, "deconstructing" a latest entry record into a number of successive entry records is often impossible. In a shared cataloging environment, however, a particular library might have holdings under only one of the titles on a latest entry record and would not be able to use the full record from a shared database.

In an attempt to overcome some of the problems with both successive and latest entry, new forms of entry were proposed. "Incorporating entry," a technique whereby each succeeding record for a title change incorporates data from the former record, was proposed by Sara Shatford Layne.[15] Jean Hirons, Judy Kuhagen, and Regina Reynolds proposed "a succession of latest entry records," another multiple record hybrid technique that also attempted to preserve the one-to-one correspondence between ISSN and records, while allowing libraries to have only one record in their catalog to represent the entire title history of an integrating publication.[16] In the end, however, the proposed new techniques seemed even more complex and cumbersome than the problem they were trying to solve. Latest entry for integrating resources was recommended and approved by the JSC.

At their annual meetings in the fall of 1998 and the fall of 1999, the directors of ISSN centers considered the problems of latest entry for the ISSN database. They felt strongly that having one set of ISSN assignment rules for serials and another for integrating resources would be very difficult for publishers to understand. Having a mixture of latest and successive entry records in the ISSN database would also make the records difficult to interpret and use. Currently, the ISSN will continue to change with title changes, and the ISSN database will continue to consist of successive entry records. Solutions to the problems facing ISSN centers that might have to create latest entry records for their national catalogs to record ISSN assignments for integrating resources are being explored.

Electronic Journals

After centuries of relative stability, journals made a leap into the online world and, in many cases, a simultaneous leap into a period of experimentation and change. No longer confined by the requirements of printing, binding, and mailing, some publishers have abandoned the concept of issues entirely and simply release each article as it becomes ready. Titles can change in an instant, and all trace of former titles can disappear, although articles may have been cited under the title that no longer appears anywhere on a journal's Web site. Journals that started out being published in issues might be redesigned to simply arrange all the articles into one alphabetical or chronological array. If that arrangement proves to be problematic, that same journal might revert to being divided into issues once again. Pity the poor cataloger who has to make a decision about whether to catalog such a journal as a serial based on whether it is divided into issues or not!

Although the model presented earlier worked well in the abstract, determining how to handle electronic journals presented another challenge. A simple solution would have been to divide e-journals into serials and integrating resources based on the presence or absence of issues. However, this would have resulted in some e-journals being cataloged using latest entry and some being cataloged using successive entry, making records for e-journals difficult to use and interpret, and causing records for print serials, all cataloged according to the rules of successive entry, to be out of sync with their online counterparts. This approach also would have made using one record for both print and online access less feasible. Furthermore, because e-journals had been observed to change from having issues to having no issues, the possibility for confusion in shared databases was a concern. After much deliberation, a closer examination of the definition of *serial* revealed a solution: E-journals consist of articles, which are, in fact, "successive parts" that do remain discrete. This solution allows print journals and e-journals to be cataloged using the same conventions of successive entry, with only one exception. The exception calls for latest entry cataloging in those thus far infrequent cases where the former title of a journal is not retained anywhere on the site. In cases such as this, it was felt that a cataloger had no choice but to use latest entry.

CHALLENGES FOR SERIALISTS

The MARC Format

Translating the new model of the bibliographic universe into codes in the MARC format that will be useful to libraries and their patrons is another formidable challenge. When a researcher comes into a library looking for information contained in continuing electronic resources, what file divisions and what labels will be most helpful? We can be sure patrons will not be looking for "integrating resources." What will they ask for: "Online publications"? "Internet stuff"? "Electronic services"?

A recently added value "s" (electronic) for the 008/23 and 006/06 form-of-item byte in MARC21 will be used to code records for resources that are electronic so that these resources may be better identified by systems in the future. But what about the code that indicates seriality? One of the primary codes in the MARC21 record that governs how records are sorted, searches limited, and files divided is the bibliographic-level byte: Leader/07. The current relevant choices are "m" for monographs and "s" for serials. Once again, the question of two categories versus three arises, because a tiered structure, such as that used in the JSC model where "continuing" is subdivided into serials and integrating resources, is not possible using only one byte.

In Discussion Paper no. 114, prepared for the June 1999 MARBI meetings, Jean Hirons outlined three options: (1) dividing resources between the current codes "m" and "s"; (2) redefining "s" to include all continuing resources; and (3) defining a new bibliographic level for integrating resources.[17] During the 1999 discussion, opinion was leaning toward either dividing resources between current codes "m" and "s," or redefining "s" to include all continuing resources. However, in a discussion paper prepared for the June 2000 MARBI meetings, Hirons proposed the definition of a new code "i" for integrating resources, to be used in conjunction with the current serials 008, which would be renamed "seriality 008." In her June 2000 discussion paper, Hirons argued that, "by following this option, MARC21 would embrace the continuing resources model: the use of the same 008 would bring out aspects of the seriality of all continuing resources, while the separate leader codes [that is, 'i' for integrating and 's' for serial] would express the form in which the seriality is realized."[18] Thus, in fact, the tiered structure of the new AACR2 model where continuing resources are subdivided into serials and integrating resources could find a MARC21 parallel. This option would allow serials to continue to be indexed, labeled, and grouped as a separate category of library material, but also allow the indexing of integrating resources if so desired. The current serials labels and infrastructure would still have relevance and meaning in library organizational structures, cooperative programs, and other library functions. Provided concerns about labeling and usage distinctions can be worked out, this MARC solution could have the advantage of preserving much of the status quo while making provisions for new publications as well.

The ISSN Network

The problem of defining *serial* in the evolving electronic world would have presented an enormous challenge for the ISSN Network, whether or not the AACR and ISBD(S) communities embraced the same challenge.

AACR revision provided the word *seriality* and a framework for the discussion; the problem was already there when the first continuing electronic resource was published. Challenges for the ISSN Network include: (1) defining and communicating to publishers what the ISSN should encompass, (2) determining the scope of the universe ISSN should attempt to control, (3) assessing and trying to meet the needs and demands of the ISSN user community, and (4) accommodating user needs with available resources or finding new resources.

To gain some insights into defining the scope of the ISSN in the digital environment and to begin planning for the future, the ISSN Network held a strategic planning session at a joint meeting of its governing board and directors in September 1999. Clifford Lynch gave the keynote address, and other experts from ISSN user communities, such as subscription agencies, libraries, and identifier groups, made presentations and provided input to discussion sessions. As a result, some different perspectives on defining *serial* in the digital world emerged. In the world of e-commerce, online linking, aggregations, and subscriptions to online services, there seemed to be a need for a much broader concept of *serial,* perhaps even broader than that being considered under the new term *continuing resource.*

In his remarks at that meeting, Clifford Lynch described the serial in the digital world not as an object or even as a series of objects, but rather as a process. To carry this thought to the extreme, Lynch referred to a stream of stock transaction quotes or the output from a digital video camera as examples of "an information process" and speculated about these kinds of processes as serials eligible to be assigned an ISSN.[19] Rollo Turner, representing subscription agents, presented a slide that read, "Definition of serial has to go!" and suggested redefining *serial* around the concept of a service. He listed several requirements for his suggested new definition of *serial:* provides a service, has a name, grows and changes rather than has parts or issues, has no end date, and can be subscribed to.[20] The enthusiasm of many of the speakers for redefining the scope of the ISSN was both encouraging and dismaying: encouraging to realize the information community seems ready for a broader definition of *serial,* but dismaying to hear that if these speakers had their way, almost everything on the Web would be a serial! On the one hand, wouldn't that be a great victory for serialists? On the other hand, how would we—serials catalogers, ISSN centers—ever cope?

Even if such a serials takeover is not imminent, the ISSN strategic planning session made it very clear that the question of seriality touches a much broader audience than the library and cataloging communities. The ISSN is at the intersection of the library and commercial worlds, and this adds yet another dimension to the seriality challenge. Because seriality is such a pervasive attribute of Web resources, and because Web resources are becoming increasingly important in commerce, the library definition of *serial* is becoming much more than a technical or theoretical issue. Economic concerns—dollars and cents—as well as potential partnerships between ISSN centers and nonlibrary organizations, may also have an influence on the ultimate utility and applicability of some of the proposals discussed here.

UNRESOLVED ISSUES

As if the present isn't challenging enough, the future promises to be even more so. It seems clear that digital resources will continue to evolve and to present new challenges for serialists. Electronic resources are a target that is moving much faster than the speed of rule revision. It might well happen that by the time rules for a new type of resource are proposed, drafted, approved, and implemented, entire new categories of electronic resources, or even the successor to the Web, will have arrived.

Recently, NSDP was confronted with a new conundrum: Is the *Wall Street Journal* for the Palm Pilot (a handheld organizer) a separate serial? Should it be assigned its own ISSN? Because of the limitations of the hardware and, more significantly, limitations imposed by the publisher's contract, the content for the Palm Pilot was not the same as the content for either the print or the online version. Although this question was not earth shattering, it promoted something of an earth-shattering vision— that of trains and buses full of commuters, each with her or his own Palm Pilot, reading everything from Ellery Queen's mystery magazine (currently available for the Palm Pilot) to the *New England Journal of Medicine* (not yet available). The corollary to that vision is one of catalogers and ISSN centers being totally overwhelmed, drowning in a sea of multitudinous multiple editions, trying in vain to keep up with each new edition for each new device, while new generations of tech-minded entrepreneurs are dreaming up more combinations and permutations of serials information. In this vision, even if no new serials were ever published, the possibility for the current number of serials and continuing resources to proliferate endlessly, like the products of an out-of-control sorcerer's apprentice, is mind-boggling.

Although these concerns probably represent an overreaction, they would seem to call for some assessment of current attempts to catalog each version of a serial as a separate bibliographic entity. Also called into question is the library community's ability to keep up with the handcrafted cataloging of electronic resources being done today. It seems inevitable that some automated or at least semiautomated means will be required to keep up with the output. Other unresolved issues will continue to challenge those who deal with serials and other continuing resources. The worlds of the library and the commercial sector are interacting more and are becoming more interdependent. Will the seriality model developed for library cataloging rules and processing have any relevance for the world of publishers and e-commerce? As resources continue to proliferate at the same time library staffs shrink, how applicable or influential will library-based standards be? The commercial world has a general understanding of the concept of *serial*, even if that understanding is not a precise one. Will the terms *continuing resource* and *integrating resource* gain the same kind of acceptance and use as the term *serial*? How can the library community promote the necessary education and understanding to guarantee their acceptance?

In addition to the commercial sector, the information-seeking public is affected more than ever by library cataloging practices. Now that library catalogs from all over the world are accessible over the Internet, the concepts and terminology developed for catalogers and library researchers may not translate well for the needs of the Internet-using public. We already know that the term *serial* is not well understood by most members of the public. How much more confused will they be by our new terms and concepts? There will be a continuing need for librarians to seek out the most appropriate labels to use in their catalogs, and the most useful and logical ways to limit searches and provide access to the materials for which information seekers are looking. It is hoped that the results of the seriality rule changes will be implemented in library catalogs in such a way as to aid in this endeavor.

It is fortunate that for serialists, the only constant is change. The Web has certainly provided a new vehicle for change and evolution in library resources. No sooner are rules and practices developed for new kinds of resources than something still newer will come along. This should not be surprising. Just like the serials and other continuing resources that serialists catalog, the challenges inherent in seriality are expected to continue indefinitely.

NOTES

1. *Anglo-American Cataloguing Rules*, 2nd ed., 1998 revision (Ottawa: Canadian Library Association; Chicago: American Library Association, 1998), 8.

2. Jean Hirons and Crystal Graham, "Issues Related to Seriality," in *The Principles and Future of AACR: Proceedings of the International Conference on the Principles and Future Development of AACR, Toronto, Ontario, Canada, October 23–25, 1997*, edited by Jean Weihs (Ottawa: Canadian Library Association; Chicago: American Library Association, 1998), 180–212.

3. Clifford Lynch and Cecilia Preston, "International Standard Serial Numbers for the Twenty-first Century: A View of the Future" (paper presented at the strategic planning session of the ISSN Network, Paris, September 1999).

4. *Anglo-American Cataloguing Rules,* 2nd ed., edited by Michael Gorman and Paul W. Winkler (Chicago: American Library Association, 1978), 8.

5. *Anglo-American Cataloguing Rules,* 2nd ed., 1998 revision, 8.

6. MARBI Proposal 93-4, "Changes to the USMARC Bibliographic Format (Computer Files) to Accommodate Online Information Resources," November 20, 1992, appendix to "Assessing Information on the Internet: Toward Providing Library Services for Computer Mediated Communication," by Martin Dillon, Erik Jul, Mark Burge, and Carol Hickey. See: http://www.oclc.org:5047/oclc/research/publications/aii/table.html

7. Hirons and Graham, "Issues Related to Seriality."

8. Jean Hirons and Regina Reynolds, "Seriality: It's Not Just for Serials Anymore," *Library Review* (Glasgow, Scotland) 48, no. 4 (1999): 163–168.

9. Jean Hirons, "Revising AACR2 to Accommodate Seriality: Report to the Joint Steering Committee for Revision of AACR," April 1999. See: http://www.nlc-bnc.ca/jsc/ser-rep0.html

10. "Revising AACR2 to Accommodate Seriality: Rule Revision Proposals," prepared by Jean Hirons and members of the CONSER AACR Review Task Force, submitted to the Joint Steering Committee for Revision of AACR, February 2000, app. D, glossary.

11. Ibid.

12. Ibid.

13. Hirons and Graham, "Issues Related to Seriality," 195–197.

14. Jean Hirons and Regina Reynolds, "Proposal to Adopt a Modified Model C," April 1998. See: http://lcweb.loc.gov/acq/conser/ModelC.html

15. Sara Shatford Layne, "Incorporating Entry: A New Concept for Cataloging Electronic Journals," May 18, 1998. See: http://lcweb.loc.gov/acq/conser/incorp.html

16. Jean Hirons, Judy Kuhagen, and Regina Reynolds, "Proposal for a Succession of Latest Entry Records," November 1998. See: http://lcweb.loc.gov/acq/conser/succlat.html

17. Discussion Paper no. 114, "Seriality and MARC21," May 14, 1999. See: http://lcweb.loc.gov/marc/marbi/dp/dp114.html

18. Discussion Paper no. 119, "Seriality and MARC21," May 1, 2000 in preparation for June 2000. See: http://lcweb. loc.gov/marc/marbi/dp/dp119.html

19. Lynch and Preston, "International Standard Serial Numbers for the Twenty-first Century."

20. Rollo Turner, "The ISSN and Serials Purchasing" (paper presented at the strategic planning session of the ISSN Network, Paris, September 1999).

2

Saddlepoints in Serials

RONALD L. LARSEN

Optimization of any system depends on assumptions of stability in the laws governing its operation. Libraries optimize their collections based on such parameters as usage profiles, available physical resources (for example, shelf space), cost of materials, and budgets. This works because each of these parameters is relatively stable. One can apply intuition, logic, and straightforward mathematics in the effort to gain the greatest return from the available resources. But what happens when stability is challenged or undermined, and traditional approaches fall short?

Spiraling serials prices in the 1980s and 1990s, coupled with the dramatic success of the World Wide Web, introduced instability into the normal processes of collection development and optimization. While libraries reacted to the cost spiral by cutting serials subscriptions and seeking greater budgets, the Web hosted experiments in alternative publishing models, most notably electronic publication. Few libraries took these experiments very seriously, arguing that the digital medium was only the most recent in a long history of media that libraries have successfully accommodated. But this one is different. The digital medium is the first medium that is fully capable of subsuming all other media. By

Originally presented as the keynote address at the First Electronic Serials Institute, "A Capital Idea: Electronic Serials from Acquisition to Access," September 26–27, 1997, Washington, D.C.

the close of the 1990s, the full impact of digital publication was still to be felt, but few doubted that its ultimate impact would be anything short of revolutionary.

Libraries—and users, publishers, service providers, and sponsors—are now in the throes of shaping the future of the infrastructure supporting our most fundamental intellectual pursuits. We are at a saddle point . . . a point at which, if we continue to do what we've always done, including optimizing our performance using traditional measures, we will lose to those who pursue more radical, perhaps even orthogonal, lines of thought. The future belongs to those who develop the revolutionary alternatives that put society on a new curve.

This chapter will explore some of these issues, not with the intent of presenting a solution or of speculating on the nature of the solution, but to better understand the forces at play. More specifically, the chapter suggests that much of our thinking about solutions is constrained by our understanding of the world, and when the world changes, we benefit from explicitly recognizing assumptions that are no longer valid, regardless of how significant they were in prior successful strategies. In fact, some of these assumptions are already being challenged in pioneering digital library research, some examples of which will be considered.

THE WEB AS CONTEXT

The explosive growth of the World Wide Web (the Web) is sufficiently well known to have become almost a cliché. But the effects are so far-reaching and fundamental that the basic data bear repeating. Though estimating the size of the Web is difficult, those who try counted more than 200 million Web pages in July 1997, and this estimate was raised to 800 million in February 1999.[1] Michael Lesk suggests that the volume of information available on the Web rivals that of the Library of Congress.[2]

The Web has demonstrated its potential to support serious scholarship, including the publication of scholarly journals. As with the introduction of other new technologies, this initially took the form of implementing the older medium in the new medium—that is, producing print journals that could be read on the screen. But it wasn't long before experiments were under way to explore the power of the Web to extend publication interactively and dynamically. A publication can now contain audio, video, simulations, models, data sets—literally anything that can be represented digitally.

Economic forces are also pressuring movement toward the Web. The purchasing power of libraries has declined tenfold over the past thirty years. Concurrently, library collections budgets have remained relatively flat. Costs for new construction of book stacks typically run between $20 and $100 per book, while scanning a book typically costs $10 to $40. Is it any mystery that administrators are less than enthusiastic about large new library construction projects?

However, with the euphoria of the Web came a slow recognition that it is also fairly disorganized and chaotic. Finding useful materials is a chore. The "signal-to-noise" ratio is disappointingly low, and even when something potentially useful is found, its provenance is largely unknown. The skills and values of librarianship are gradually becoming recognized as vital to tame the Web and help it realize its potential for scholarly communication. The rigor commonplace to research libraries must become commonplace on the Web. The ideal of global collections representing the best and most current information available is achievable, but not easily at hand. And many of the challenges are not technical at all, but relate to complex national and international legal and economic contexts. Currently, for example, the Uniform Computer Information Transactions Act (UCITA) is being considered by several state legislatures, and many within the library community are justifiably concerned about the effects of this legislation on libraries' ability to manage digital materials in their collections.[3]

PERSISTENT TECHNOLOGICAL ASSUMPTIONS

Old habits are hard to break. I began my computing career writing assembly language programs for the Apollo program's real-time mission support systems. Memory was precious, and we took substantial pride in being able to wring every extraneous byte out of an algorithm. Using four bytes to represent a year was unthinkable. I mention this because, somewhere down deep inside of me, I still think of computational resources as something to be managed, if not rationed. Although the $3,000 laptop computer I am now using to compose this chapter has a hundred times the memory of the multimillion-dollar Apollo system of the early 1970s, it still takes conscious effort for me to break through the "scarce resources" assumption.

Technology is like that. It destroys old assumptions, but those assumptions linger in the minds of those who lived through their era of validity. It is only by explicitly identifying these assumptions and questioning their current validity that we can exorcize them. During the planning stage for the second phase of the federal digital libraries research program (DLI2), a serious attempt was made to do just that—to identify technical and nontechnical assumptions that implicitly influence our thinking but whose validity may be subject to challenge.[4] This chapter will explore eight such assumptions. The challenge is to recognize each assumption for what it is and to consider the ramifications of its potential obsolescence.

ASSUMPTION 1

Resources Are Scarce

When resources are scarce or costly, their utilization is carefully managed, monitored, and often mediated. Commercial information services in libraries, for example, are commonly mediated by a reference librarian, primarily because of a combination of cost, complexity, and the variety of the underlying services available. Mediation limits access and controls use. Done properly, the mediator not only manages the quantitative use of the resource, but also provides a value-added qualitative service based on knowledge and experience. But the Web has changed much of this. Low-cost computing and communications open new avenues for information services that we are only beginning to explore.

In a world of plenty, one must rethink the manner of interaction between the user and the information source, and rethink where mediation is appropriate. Too many systems are still built on an underlying assumption of narrowband, text-based user interfaces. The typical query, for example, is a sequence of, perhaps, twenty to fifty characters and is rooted in dial-up technologies capable of delivering a few hundred characters per second. Today's networks are many orders of magnitude faster than this, and the networks of the future will be faster still. Broadband, active networks accessed through high-performance workstations offer the potential of semantically and contextually rich query expression and interaction with information spaces. And low-cost infrastructure offers the opportunity for products and services never before envisioned.

It does not necessarily follow, however, that more bandwidth and higher levels of system performance will improve productivity. Experience on the Web suggests the situation is more complex. Broadband duplex communication not only expands the user's access to potentially useful information, but also expands the user's availability (and potential vulnerability) to others. The risks include increased exposure to materials of marginal interest as well as to materials with no enduring value whatsoever.

It is likely that twenty years from now, computing and communication resources essentially will be unlimited, particularly in comparison to that which is commonly available today. It is nearly impossible to anticipate how these resources may be used. In 1980, I participated in a National Aeronautics and Space Administration/American Society for Engineering Education (NASA/ASEE) summer study considering the progress that could be achieved in space exploration and utilization over a fifty-year period, unconstrained by fiscal realities. The only constraints were those of scientific and engineering discipline. Anything proposed had to be technically feasible (not necessarily affordable). With the traditional resource constraints of time and money largely removed, the only remaining constraint was the intellectual power required to envision a different future. What emerged was an extraordinarily creative investigation of interstellar exploration, lunar and asteroid mining, and earth resources monitoring.[5]

Computing and communication resources are not scarce, nor is money necessarily the constraining resource we typically assume. Overcoming this assumption, however, requires recognition of the significant change in the landscape as well as recognition of the difficulty of understanding the profound effects of technologies that are advancing exponentially. The inhibiting force has shifted from people acting as gatekeepers to technology, to ubiquitous technology competing for the attention of people who can exploit it. The shortage of information technology (IT) workers exacerbates this situation and has been widely documented.[6]

ASSUMPTION 2

Measurement Yields Improvement

Metrics are very popular as guides for improving human productivity, in areas from research to routine operations. Wise measurement using good metrics can be valuable. It focuses attention on incremental improvements. Human nature assures that behavior will largely conform to the real or perceived rewards. And when the rewards are directly coupled to a measured quantity, then we can be reasonably assured that behavior will adapt to move the measurement in the more rewarding direction. Qualitative breakthroughs are more complex and difficult to obtain (hence, they're called breakthroughs), and are rarely the product of metrics-based evaluation. In information retrieval, for example, precision and recall have driven the research and development agenda for decades, even though these criteria were developed and are more appropriate for batch-oriented single-try queries. Despite the attention to precision and recall, no search engine comes close to human performance.[7]

Except under rather contrived test circumstances, it is not rigorously clear what precision and recall even mean in an environment as dynamic as the Web. Under the auspices of the Defense Advanced Research Projects Agency (DARPA), the Dlib Forum Working Group on Metrics is charged with developing new metrics and guides to evaluate progress in digital library technologies, including information retrieval.[8] More than one year into the effort, the group is recognizing the many dimensions of the problem and the complexity that ensues in trying to define and measure progress rigorously.

Although measurement can be very helpful, it can also slow progress by focusing too much attention on too limited a criterion. To bind a community rigidly to metrics grounded in prior generations is to foreclose serious exploration of qualitative breakthroughs.

ASSUMPTION 3

Information Seeking Begins with Search

Search engines owe much of their historic development to an implicit assumption of a well-organized, relatively homogeneous collection (the type of collection one would typically find in a library or commercial abstracting and indexing database, for example). The Web violates this assumption. Information sources and resources on the Web are highly diverse, distributed, and heterogeneous, with greatly varying content and quality. Search loses its effectiveness as information volume grows and source heterogeneity increases. Increased document and information density resists discrimination by traditional search technologies.

Understanding search as an end-game strategy exposes the assumption that the user has gotten to the point where specific results can be specified, sought, and identified. Until relatively late in an information-seeking activity, this is not necessarily the case. Attributes other than lexical similarity need to be considered. Semantics is certainly an obvious and important area, but it needs to be considered broadly, encompassing context-based, value-based, and cross-media semantics. Building a more powerful search engine merely focuses more intently on the back end of the information-seeking process, when the more striking contemporary problems may exist at the front end.

Metaphorically speaking, consider a search engine a sieve through which sand is passing, filtering out just the right grains. The inevitable result of increasing the quantity of sand through the sieve is an increasing quantity of sand that meets the filtering constraints of the sieve, resulting in more grains of sand of marginal relevance remaining for later consideration. As information density increases, a search engine can do little more than register all the objects that share a terminological attribute with the stated query.

As one unscientific example, in 1998 I did a series of searches using the search terms "DARPA Frank Fernandez." At the time, Frank Fernandez was the new director of DARPA. I imagined this query to be the type of naïve, simple query that one might make before visiting DARPA or as background for preparation of a proposal. In this one sample test, we can get a taste of the variability among Web search engines, summarized in table 1.

TABLE 1   Summary of Results from Naïve Search
            "DARPA Frank Fernandez"

Search Engine	Observation
AltaVista	First 1 of 37,880 correct
Excite	First 2 of 522,725 correct
Google	First 15 of 43 correct
HotBot	First 3 of 118 correct (2 conference agendas)
Infoseek	First correct return was 22nd of 15,294
Lycos	One out of the first 5 was correct
Webcrawler	First 1 of 18,958 correct; 9 of first 25 correct
WebDirectory	First 3 of 522,725 correct
Yahoo!	First 3 of 14 correct (2 conference agendas)

It is important here to understand that most of these search engines were developed independent of federal support, but many drew from results produced in federally sponsored research, particularly the multiagency Tipster Text Program.[9] The Google search engine is of interest as one that was a more direct product of Stanford University's participation in the Digital Libraries Initiative, and one that applied principles of citation counts to estimate the relevance of a particular Web site to a query. For this particular query, Google arguably performed the best among the sampled engines, although that result should not be considered a generalizable result or a criticism of any of the others, as each one optimizes on different criteria particular to its respective market. But the qualitative differences among them are not readily apparent to the user.

Google's indexes use reverse citation counts to weight Web pages. Pages that are referenced more frequently by other Web pages are more highly regarded than those that are referenced less. This is an early attempt, and one of the few that is actually operational, at establishing an implicit, content-based value index. It is among the first entries into value-based search that has been commercialized.

Today's search engines appear to be effective largely because the information space over which they are operating is statistically very large. With a sufficient investment of human knowledge, persistence, and patience, useful results are frequently achieved in monolingual (usually English) searches. But information seeking should end with search—it should not begin with it. It may begin with visualization, perceiving the global information space at an abstract level, then proceed through navigation and bounding operations to scope the space of interest. Search may then follow effectively. Signal processing metaphors (for example, wavelet analysis, to be considered later) may provide insight into issues of semantic abstraction. Information seekers need a rich and varied toolbox of filters on multidimensional measures of content, context, and value that cross media boundaries. But stronger theoretical foundations may be required than are presently available.

The state of the art in information access and utilization today can be thought of in relatively linear terms. The process begins with the formulation of a query. The query is the input to an information retrieval process that generates candidate documents. Various document-processing algorithms can be run against this set to understand it without studying it exhaustively. Topic detection algorithms can recognize with reasonable precision the occurrence of stories about specified topics.[10] Named entities, such as names of people, places, and things, dates, or events can be extracted with very good recognition accuracy.[11] Modest success has been achieved automatically summarizing documents, although much remains to be done.[12] Each of these processes introduces errors, and these errors tend to propagate through the analysis, leaving compound errors of significant magnitude by the time the process is complete. Relevance feedback improves information retrieval performance by about 50 percent, but no analogous improvements have been suggested for the other analysis steps, and little consideration has been given to understanding how the various processes interact.

ASSUMPTION 4

The Goal Is to Find an Answer

Much of the preceding discussion suggests or implies that the objective is to find an answer and, by inference, that with appropriately powerful tools, the answer can be found. Attempts at improving performance by increasingly powerful and complex search have yielded only marginal returns, while producing bewildering user interface complexity. Alternatives to search are needed, especially in the early stages of information exploration, that recast the objective as perceiving the information space at variable resolution and levels of abstraction. Information visualization is a powerful metaphor for understanding complex information spaces, and the literature is rich.[13] Battelle Pacific Northwest National Laboratory's SPIRE system provides one example of the application of powerful visualization tools to navigate large and complex collections of documents.[14]

ASSUMPTION 5

The Answer Is in the Information

Search and the related analytical tools considered up to this point presuppose that the "answer" can be found in the information. That which is sought, however, may not lie exclusively in information artifacts. Relationships that require the collaborative expertise of individuals interacting with information may be missed. Relaxing this assumption encourages interoperability among searching, authoring, and collaboration facilities, and recognizes their interdependence in complex problem solving.

ASSUMPTION 6

English Suffices

Most of the tools available today on the Web were built with English as the target language. As the Web continues to expand, however, its growth rate in non-English-speaking countries exceeds the rate of growth in the United States. This is due in part to the earlier and greater penetration of the Web in the United States. Estimates made in 1999 suggested that the number of non-English-language Web pages would exceed English Web pages midyear.[15] The user relying entirely on English-language materials risks missing nearly half the potentially available information on the Web. Such reliance also introduces a misleading and potentially dangerous Anglocentric bias. A comprehensive approach must include the ability to locate, acquire, and utilize information resources in unfamiliar languages. This is the focus of DARPA's research program in Translingual Information Detection, Extraction, and Summarization (TIDES).[16] As of 1999, search engines working across select language boundaries performed about half as well as those working within one language.

ASSUMPTION 7

Information Is a Commodity

Traditional economic models treat information as a commodity. It is created, packaged, purchased, loaned, copied, and sold. Containers of information (for example, books, magazines, newspapers) are treated largely as if they actually are the information. The economic model for print is typically based on a pay-to-read model. Copyright provisions governing fair use and first sale make the model fit the free access and lending requirements of libraries.

Information on the Web is different. Authors pay to have their material read, by assuming the cost and liability of putting their materials on the Web, and readers expect information to be free. This pay-to-publish model is feasible because of the low barrier to entry for Web-based publishing. The ease with which authors can do this calls into question the traditional role of publishers. With a diminishing need for the manufacture and distribution of physical formats, the publisher's role is more clearly one of adding value to the information itself. Individual authors can easily put their materials on the Web, accessible on a global basis, but the user seeking quality information still derives value from vetted sources, and this is the primary role of a publisher. A publisher can also take the initiative in encouraging authors to write on particular topics and can serve as an informed broker to information.

The business model for Web-based publishing remains in flux, however. What is the role of payment? Is it a special case of a broader model in a networked environment? It is certainly the case that a large and growing body of important information is made available at the cost of the author rather than the reader. Consider, for example, government information, research reports, business reports, and investment information. Advertising is increasingly becoming part of the payment model for the Web, but even what we conventionally consider to be advertising is shifting toward a push model of information customized to the interests and preferences of the customer, and offers the opportunity to redefine conventional notions of advertising.

When information is increasingly given away, what is lost and what is gained? Advancing technology routinely displaces one set of products and technologies with another. Might this happen with print? Print costs continue to rise. The number of scientific journals continues to grow as disciplines divide and subdivide. Collections budgets remain relatively flat. Authors increasingly put preprints on their Web sites for free access by anyone. Preprint servers become central to scientific communication within disciplines. Publication delays of months or years in print are eclipsed by publication delays of hours or days on the Web.

Electronic publication leads to vigorous real-time dialogue, debate, and collaboration. The trends in print and electronic publication could well be diverging. Both will likely survive, but in doing so, each will need to accommodate the other, with print publication making the larger accommodation.

How will scientific publication evolve? Text remains the most effective vehicle for widespread scientific communication, and paper remains the most effective medium for presenting text. Large volumes of print are difficult to read on a screen, and materials designed for effective presentation on the screen typically do not translate well to print. Most of the successes to date have capitalized primarily on timeliness of publication, although the potential of the digital medium to present dynamic interactive content irreproducible on the printed page remains compelling.

The Web reduces the barriers of entry to publishing by eliminating the printing costs and enabling global distribution at very low cost. Self-publishing becomes available and accessible to anyone with modest skills and a personal computer. Roles previously filled by middlemen seem less necessary. Publishers and computer centers are examples of these middle roles, but the effects extend beyond these to secondary information providers (for example, abstracting and indexing services) and catalogers. Although the functions provided by these middle-layer providers will continue to be viable, the question is: How are the services provided? Must they be provided by a professional skilled in that particular area? Is this even affordable? Can an automated process deliver an acceptable level of service? Can the original author provide the entire end-to-end service?

The Internet is, of course, the fundamental infrastructure upon which much of this depends. The technological infrastructure has shown itself to be scalable and reasonably resilient, although it is subject to a range of other threats that have yet to be fully understood. Among these threats are opportunities for fraud and libel, spamming, cyberterrorism, pornography, and sabotage to critical societal infrastructures.

ASSUMPTION 8

People Can (or Must) Do It All

The information technology (IT) revolution is transforming virtually every aspect of society. Well into the twenty-first century, IT will be the central force shaping almost every institution in society, including private sector companies, educational and cultural institutions, and government agencies. IT will transform the way human beings work, conduct business, and entertain themselves.

IT is pervasive in its impact because it can dramatically enhance an organization's ability to obtain, share, and structure information; by so doing, it enables the organization to increase continually its base of knowledge as well as to enhance its efficiency and competitiveness. Because of IT's vast power to effect change, it has become a major growth industry worldwide.

With the rapid advancement of IT, the world economy is being transformed into an information economy. Just as capital and energy replaced land and labor some two hundred years ago, codified information and knowledge are now replacing capital and energy as the primary wealth-creating assets. Nowhere is this change more important than in its effect on the nature of human work. The laborers of the twentieth century who transformed and utilized physical resources are being replaced by knowledge workers—people skilled in interpreting and transforming information. The emerging information economy is growing two-and-a half times as fast as the goods economy, and the IT workforce is growing six times faster than the total workforce, without meeting the demand. Across the nation, there continues to be a desperate call for more IT professionals. A 1998 survey in the state of Washington found that "projected demand for information technology program graduates outstrips locally educated supply by a factor of at least four at the community and technical colleges . . . , by a factor of over eight for bachelor's-level graduates at the public and private 4-year colleges and universities, and by a factor of two for graduate-level programs."[17]

In addition to the need for "new hires," there is a strong demand for sophisticated IT education and training for the workforce in place, and for professionals who are concerned with acquiring and keeping their IT skills current. Although many universities, corporations, and states are increasing their emphasis on IT workforce development, the type of restructuring that is occurring as a result of the Web's influence on publishing can be expected to impact other areas of our society and economy as well.

ASSUMPTIONS VERSUS REALITIES

The preceding assumptions were once valid. They reflected an informed understanding of the state of information technology and its relationship to society, and greatly simplified the process of developing new systems and capabilities. But these assumptions have been eclipsed by progress, and have been replaced by a new set of realities that are considered here.

REALITY 1

Resources Are Plentiful; Time Is Scarce

The 1990s witnessed explosive growth of the Web, expanding dramatically the information that is accessible and potentially usable to a wide variety of consumers. But identifying, acquiring, and interpreting relevant information pose enormous problems. Although an exponentially growing volume of information is potentially available to one with copious time and substantial diligence, digital library research makes this information accessible and usable to those confronting information-intensive activities without the luxury of time.

REALITY 2

Measurement Is Good; Innovation Is Better

Digital libraries are facing a number of significant technology challenges that force them to confront old assumptions. Three of these are real-time ingest, federation of distributed repositories, and translingual interaction. Issues of ingest and federation have attracted attention within the Digital Library Initiative, but translingual interaction is a relatively new emphasis, and one that is central to DARPA's TIDES program. Real-time ingest includes the capture, interpretation, cataloging, and indexing of high-rate multimedia data flows in real time. Federated repositories require organizing heterogeneous distributed information sources into comprehensive discipline-oriented, user-accessible repositories. Translingual interaction includes automatically accessing and using information among multiple natural languages. Translingual services have attracted little attention within the Web community and even less attention in digital library research. The Tipster Text Program fostered work in cross-lingual information retrieval, but effective utilization of information occurring in different languages presents a broad array of daunting challenges beyond mere retrieval.

Consider language-independent information access and utilization. Given a query in one language, one could use a bilingual dictionary to translate each of the terms of the query into the target language, and then treat that as the active query. Unfortunately, there is no one-to-one mapping of words and their uses between languages. A term in one language may map into multiple terms in the target language, depending on the sense of the original term or on alternative definitions it may have in the source language. Although only one of these terms will be correct in the target language, there is no way to determine this using only term translation with dictionaries. Hence we encounter the "fanout problem." Each term of the source-language query produces multiple terms in the target-language query. Information retrieval in the target language will now suffer significant deterioration in precision because of the introduction of irrelevant terms. Solving this problem typically relies on techniques of semantic disambiguation, requiring substantial knowledge of each of the languages to be embedded in the information retrieval system. Until recently, the technologies required here were largely the domain of automated language translation.

Given a perfect machine translation system, one could translate the query somewhat better, but no perfect machine translation systems exist. Good machine translation is available for only a handful of language pairs, but there are thousands of languages in the world, and hundreds of truly significant ones in the context of the Web and digital publication. Machine translation is traditionally a carefully handcrafted activity among linguists and computer scientists. A growing body of research suggests that nonlinguistic analysis of language (for example, statistical analysis of large corpora) may provide significant shortcuts that are tactically useful for finding and interpreting foreign-language resources, and strategically useful in developing an understanding of a new target language. Given a sufficiently large parallel corpus and a reference grammar for one of the languages, one can construct a grammar for the target language. These techniques will not be sufficient for creating artistic translations of poetry or literature, but they can be effective at identifying relevant materials and extracting facts and relationships that could be critical to the information user. The research challenge is to improve the quality of the derived grammars and translations with smaller parallel corpora, and making greater use of comparable corpora. Comparable corpora are bodies of material about the same topic but not derived directly from each other. World news provides a good contemporary example of material that can be considered comparable corpora.

REALITY 3

Incremental Advances Are Useful; Orders-of-Magnitude Leaps Are Transforming

Although language is one of the more obvious barriers to broader utilization of the growing body of information resources on the Web, it is not the only one. During my recent tenure at DARPA, I identified nine directions and goals for research necessary to bring much of the power of the research library to the Web, where by *power* I mean the basic infrastructure of rigorous catalogs, indexes, abstracts, and reference support. The overarching goal was to ultimately establish a globally interoperable digital library infrastructure that would routinely support multimodal access to multimedia materials in multiple languages. Multimodal access entails the ability to combine, substitute for, and smoothly move between various modes of interaction, including keyboard/mouse, voice, gaze, and gesture. The directions and goals are summarized in table 2.

TABLE 2   Research Directions and Goals

Capability	*Present*	*Goal*
Federated Repositories	Tens (Custom)	Thousands (Generic)
Items per Repository	Thousands	Millions
Size of "large" item	1 MB	100 MB
Typical response time	10 seconds	100 milliseconds
Mode	Play and Display	Correlate and Manipulate
Interoperability	Syntactic	Semantic
Filters	Bibliographic	Contextual
Language	Multilingual	Translingual
Content extraction	Forms and Tags	Text, image, audio

Federated Repositories

A federated repository is a repository of digital objects that is a member of a group of repositories that share a common purpose. The most obvious common purpose would be a shared topic area or academic discipline, although other relationships could give rise to a federation. The concept of a federation means that the participants typically share a common interest, and that this common interest is expressed as a set of distributed resources that are implemented, managed, and maintained in a distributed fashion, yet appear to the user as a coherent collection. One of the better examples is the Networked Computer Science Technical Reference Library (NCSTRL).[18] NCSTRL is a federated repository of technical reports and other gray literature produced by more than one hundred computer science departments in universities worldwide. NCSTRL was built as a federal research project intended to test the underlying concepts and to develop an operational pilot project. Although it has been successful in its goals, it has also pointed to the need for a scalable, generic, widely deployable set of tools for federated repositories. The goal is to make development of a federated repository as easy as development of a Web site today.

Items per Repository

Each of these repositories is relatively small, typically holding several thousand items. Items are largely Web renderings of print materials with relatively few pieces; hence, the overall conceptual structure of items is simple. But as Web publication advances and the publications themselves become more complex, involving many components in many forms interacting in currently unimaginable ways, repositories will need to handle such complexity. Just as research libraries today typically handle millions of objects, federated repositories will need to scale to comparable capacity.

Size of "Large" Item

Given that most items in NCSTRL are renderings of text documents, their size is typically a few megabytes. Repositories are already coping with multimedia materials on an order of magnitude greater than this, and we can expect this trend to continue. Our understanding of what constitutes a "large" object will continue to evolve, but we can already foresee the need to work with objects that are hundreds of megabytes in size.

Response Time

Human performance using online systems and information is strongly correlated with system response time. The Web suffers from highly variable response time. Further, common experience suggests that the size and complexity of Web pages are growing faster than the typical user's available bandwidth, resulting in perceived response times that may actually be getting larger. Optimal human performance is achieved when system performance is closer to human response time. Consistent system response of one to a few tenths of a second matches human performance well, but most users today experience response times more like ten seconds. Improving response time itself is a complex problem with many dimensions. Brute-force approaches to expand the physical availability of bandwidth are necessary and valuable, but not sufficient. Careful protocol design, intelligent caching, and ergonomic design of information resources and their delivery are also required.

Mode

Information delivery and utilization on the Web, although far more interactive than print publication and broadcast media, are still dominated by a mode of operation in which the user accesses material produced by another and proceeds to read it, display it, or play it. The Web does little to help the user correlate the content of one resource with another, and the ability to manipulate materials, without compromising intellectual property rights, is only now beginning to emerge. Research on multivalent documents has demonstrated the potential for effectively manipulating, annotating, and sharing marked-up versions of Web resources without compromising intellectual property, but much remains to be done.[19]

Interoperability

Interoperable systems are fundamental to the success of the Web. Without basic agreement on signaling, communication protocols, markup languages, and metadata, for example, little could truly be accomplished. But the growth and value of the Web have brought recognition of a need for higher levels of interoperability. Interoperability standards today are largely syntactic with structural semantics. Great care attends the syntax of communication. Relatively simple grammars are used, and the meaning of particular encoding is rigorously specified. As resources and services on the Web grow, a strong need is emerging for semantic interoperability in which interacting services can understand each other sufficiently to negotiate terms and deliver interoperable services. Semantic interoperability remains a fundamental challenge with profound impact on the long-term effectiveness of digital libraries and serials publication.[20]

Filters

The earlier discussion on assumptions expressed the view that search engines are an inadequate tool to cope with the growth of information on the Web. Search engines work primarily as an "information pull" device, responding to an explicit query. Filters serve a similar function for "pushed" information, or information that has come to us without explicit request. Filters interrogate specified fields of material to determine to which category it belongs. The user is expected to have set up sufficiently meaningful categories so that filters improve overall productivity by separating items of high interest and priority from those that may be disposed of without further action. These are static settings. A filter that can dynamically adapt to a user's task and focus of attention, or "context," would be substantially more valuable, but remains a research challenge.

Language

The Web is already multilingual. Standards such as Unicode have been effective at dealing with issues of multilingual character representation. If materials in an abundance of languages are to provide value to an individual, however, that individual needs the tools to find them, interpret them, and interact with their authors. A Web with these capabilities is a "translingual" Web. This is a major research challenge and the subject of current research through DARPA's TIDES program and the joint National Science Foundation/European Union Multilingual Information Access (MLIA) program.[21]

Researchers at the University of Southern California Information Sciences Institute (USC-ISI) conducted an insightful experiment into translingual Web tools in 1998.[22] Massive fires were burning across Indonesia and little was known about their origin or appropriate steps to counter them. Bahasa is the native language of most of the people in that area, but few in the United States are competent in that language. Hence, information available on the Web was largely useless to non-Bahasa speakers who might have an interest in the unfolding crisis. USC-ISI researchers in computational linguistics and information retrieval (themselves unfamiliar with Bahasa) sought parallel corpora between Bahasa and English. They found an electronic Bible in Bahasa and a bilingual dictionary, but little else. Working with these limited resources, within six weeks they had constructed a rudimentary translation system based largely on word substitution, and integrated this translator with a Web search engine and a document summarizer. The resultant experimental prototype, called Multilingual Summarization and Translation (MuST), was made available as a Web service and used experimentally by those investigating the Indonesian fires. It enabled the user to enter an English query that was then translated into Bahasa and passed on to a search engine. Results were automatically translated into English and summarized for the user. Although an early and primitive step in the development of translingual Web services, delivering less than perfect results, this experiment demonstrated feasibility of the concept and was seminal to the subsequent TIDES program.

Content Extraction

Information users who rely on large volumes of material that have a relatively short period of relevance (for example, news reports) are increasingly seeking (and relying on) techniques for automated content extraction. The standard approaches to content extraction, derived largely from database technology, rely on structured forms and tagged data fields. They are not effective for less-structured and more-dynamic information. Good results have been achieved recently on automatically extracting information important to understanding events-based textual reports, such as the names of people, places, and things, dates, and fundamental relationships among entities.[23] Research in this area focuses on four problems of increasing difficulty: named entity recognition, coreference identification, template element extraction, and scenario template completion. Examples of named entities are people, organizations, locations, dates, times, currencies, and other numerical measures, such as percentages. The coreference problem is one of identifying all mentions of a given entity, either directly or by indirect reference (for example, he, she, it). Template elements are intended to extract basic information related to a named entity (for example, Bill Clinton is president of the United States). Scenario templates relate event information to named entities (for example, Bill Clinton was elected president of the United States in 1992 and 1996). Promising results are also being achieved in coupling entity recognition capabilities with speech recognition to interpret news broadcasts and to identify and track news reports on specific topics automatically.[24] A broad range of content extraction capabilities is required across the full range of multimedia. Fundamental to this research is recognition that data of the highest interest will be highly dynamic, largely unstructured, and often noisy.

Although progress is being made in extracting noun forms and correlating them with events, we are a long way from building systems that can interpret, or even represent, a broad range of semantics or meaning expressed in text. Humans are very good at compressing a story into temporal or spatial constraints. Consider, for example, the imminent meeting where you might be called upon to report on an impending situation about which you have very little knowledge, but for which you know someone who has deeper knowledge. A quick call to that person might result in a two-minute summary of the situation—all that you need to know to get through the meeting. Later, however, you might return to that individual to learn more. Perhaps this takes an hour or two. Still later, you might develop a keen interest in the situation and spend long periods of time with the individual, learning many of the details. How do people do this so naturally? It is as if we have an innate ability to abstract the right level of detail to fit the constraints of a given situation.

Researchers at Battelle Pacific Northwest National Laboratory are applying wavelet transform theory derived in signal processing to interpret and portray the underlying semantic structure and flow of documents at multiple levels of resolution.[25] In an approach they call "top-icography," they treat text as the underlying signal against which various wavelet transforms are applied, with the objective of characterizing the content and flow of document text at varying levels of detail. Their hypothesis is that wavelet transforms can be effective at analyzing textual narrative in the frequency domain, enabling the automatic representation and extraction of thematic changes within the document. Although this approach is in a very early stage of development, it represents an increasing interest in tools that expand an individual's capability to assess rapidly and effectively the content of massive documents and collections of documents.

This interest stems directly from the explosive growth in information accessible from open sources, such as the Web, and its relevance to time critical activities. Consider, for example, the role that digital libraries played in a very real crisis situation. In the winter of 1997, floods ravaged much of California. Property loss was immense and the Department of Water Resources (DWR) was struggling to stay on top of the situation. Fortuitously, digital library researchers at the University of California, Berkeley had partnered with the DWR several years earlier to develop an environmental digital library for the state. Documents with dam specifications, fish populations, and related water resources data existed only on paper, but were digitized as part of the project. Berkeley researchers' development of multivalent document technologies demonstrated how these scanned materials could be searched, tabulated, restructured, reformatted, annotated, and otherwise enhanced for a variety of unforeseen purposes. This capability became fundamental to the DWR's management of the flood crisis. It gave DWR real-time access to critical data statewide and enabled the department to post near real-time situation updates to flood workers, the news media, and the public. The digital library supports a wide range of materials, including geographic data, aerial imagery, photographs, text, and numeric data, and is building tools for correlating information across media types (for example, geographic data overlaid on aerial imagery).[26]

We do not need a crisis, however, to witness the potential of digital libraries and electronic publication. Digital library researchers at the University of Illinois, Urbana-Champaign (UIUC) have been developing statistically based techniques of semantic indexing for navigating, accessing, and using massive text collections. In a 1998 experiment reported in *Science* magazine, UIUC researchers used their Interspace technologies to develop an alternative means of organizing and accessing the National Institutes of Health's MEDLINE database of biomedical research.[27] The database consists of more than 10 million articles that have been manually indexed for MEDLINE. MEDLINE is widely regarded as the premier information resource for the medical community, but it is primarily a research resource rather than a practitioner's reference. One participant in the UIUC experiment, Dr. Richard Berlin, a surgeon and medical director at Health Alliance, noted that "if you work hard at it and you have a lot of time, you can usually, but not always, find the information that you are looking for." Another participant, Dr. Jonathan Silverstein, a surgeon at the University of Illinois, Chicago, was quoted as saying MEDLINE, with the semantic indexing provided by UIUC, was "wonderful. I'm now getting far more useful information out of MEDLINE, and I'm getting it in a time frame . . . while the patient [is] in my office."[28]

REALITY 4

Information Technology Enables; Information Empowers

The common thread running through each of the preceding examples reflects the fundamental characteristics of society's use of information and the Web today. It is characterized on the one hand by an exponential growth of both sources and services, and on the other by a critical requirement for timeliness and accuracy by decision makers who have insufficient time and attention to cope with the flood of information. Information users increasingly need improved capabilities to discover new information, filter it for relevance, and fuse it with other materials. They need to be able to interact seamlessly across multiple media and languages using multiple modes of expression. The technological solutions brought to bear on these problems need to be highly adaptable to a wide range of situations, given the absence of a priori knowledge of what information will prove relevant to a specific situation. But this is the classic library reference problem and the very reason libraries exist. The partnership of those with technological prowess and creativity and those with the skills and techniques of librarianship may form the critical alliance required to develop effective tools capable of taming the flood of information on the Web.

Digital libraries will become a major component of a global information infrastructure, in which individuals and organizations can efficiently and effectively identify, assemble, correlate, manipulate, and disseminate information resources, regardless of the medium in which the information may exist. Digital libraries make no assumptions about commonality of language or discipline between problem solver and the information space, but instead, strive to provide tools to navigate and manipulate a multilingual, multidisciplinary world. It is assumed, however, that task context, user values, and information provenance are critical elements in the information-seeking process.

The accelerating pace of world events coupled with the expansion of the Web underscores the urgency of developing adaptive technology to rapidly acquire, filter, organize, and manipulate large collections of multimedia and active digital objects in a global distributed network to provide the ability to investigate and assess time-critical, multifaceted situations. Information management requirements in support of crisis management and humanitarian relief typically push the current boundaries by two orders of magnitude in quantitative parameters, such as numbers of coordinated repositories, sizes of collections, sizes of objects, and timeliness of response. In addition, qualitative improvement is required in the creation, correlation, and manipulation of information from multiple disciplines and in multiple languages.

REALITY 5

Orders-of-Magnitude Leaps
Begin Incrementally

Today's information retrieval systems rely largely on indexing the text of documents. Though this can be effective in bounded domains in which the usage and definition of words are shared, performance suffers when materials from multiple disciplines are represented in the same collection, or when disparate acquisition or selection policies are active. Rather than being the exception, however, this is typically the rule (especially on the Web). Techniques for mapping between structured vocabularies begin to address this problem for disciplines that are fortunate enough to have a formalized vocabulary.[29]

Techniques are needed that look beyond words, however, to meanings and concepts. Automated techniques for collection categorization are required, and UIUC's Interspace project has reported substantial success using statistical approaches on large corpora.[30]

Query languages and tools seek to identify materials in a given collection that are similar to the characteristics expressed in a given query. These characteristics focus on the information artifact and have yet to consider nonbibliographic attributes that might focus a search more tightly. Examples include identifying the types of individuals who have been reading specific material, ascertaining the value they associated with it, and determining the paths they traversed to find it.[31]

The navigational metaphor has become ubiquitous for information seeking in the network environment, but highly effective and facile tools for visualizing and navigating these complex information spaces remain to be fully developed. Incorporation of concept spaces and semantic category maps into visualization tools is a promising improvement. Concept spaces and semantic category maps are illustrative of statistically based techniques to analyze collections, to associate vocabulary with topics, to suggest bridging terms between clusters of documents, and to portray the clusters of related documents in a multidimensional, navigable space, enabling both high-level abstraction and drill-down to specific documents.[32] Additional approaches, including alternatives to the navigational metaphor, are needed.

Scalability and interoperability continue to be major challenges. The objective is to build scalable repository technology that supports the federation of thousands of repositories, presenting to the user a coherent collection consisting of millions of related items, and to do this rigorously across many disciplines. As the size and complexity of information objects increase, so does the bandwidth required to utilize these objects. Real-time interactivity is required for the time-critical assessment of complex situations, pushing the bandwidth requirements yet higher. As this capability emerges, broadband interoperability becomes feasible, in which the user's inputs are no longer constrained to a few keystrokes, with the return channel carrying the high-volume materials. Research is required to explore the nature of such broadband interoperability and the opportunities it brings to raise the effectiveness of the information user.

Human attention has become the critical resource. The challenge is to provide the most relevant materials to the user in the least amount of time by providing a powerful array of tools and automated facilities. Real-time correlation and manipulation of a broad array of information resources are critical to this task. Correlation of diverse information types, such as geographical information (for example, maps and aerial imagery) with event-related materials (for example, documents and news reports), is becoming increasingly important. The GeoWorlds project is integrating geographically oriented digital library technology with scalable collection analysis to demonstrate this evolving approach to time-critical applications in a collaborative setting.[33]

It will come as little surprise to library professionals that the digital library research agenda can be broadly structured into context- or task-independent repository-based functions and user- or usage-dependent analysis activities. This is, after all, largely the way libraries have traditionally divided their activities. These categories can be further subdivided into the following components:

Repository functions

Enrollment and security to provide the registration, access controls, and rights management facilities required to support secure applications in an open network environment.

Classification and federation to advance the capability to automate the acquisition, classification, and indexing of information resources among distributed repositories.

Distributed service assurance to address the vital concerns of matching user interaction styles and needs to system performance capabilities. This direction also pushes the boundaries of interactivity over broadband networks.

Analysis activities

Semantic interoperability to extend the user's ability to interact with diverse information from distributed sources at the conceptual level.

Translingual interaction to provide the information user the facility for identifying and evaluating the relevance and value of foreign-language materials to a particular query, without assuming the user has any proficiency in the foreign language.

Information visualization and filtering to navigate complex multidimensional information spaces, and user-customizable, value-oriented filters to rank information consistent with the context of the task being performed.

CONCLUSION

The information user's attention has become the critical resource. Digital library research and, by extension, electronic serials development need to provide the technological capability to get the most out of the user's attention in the least amount of time. In short, the rigor and organization normally associated with a research library need to be virtually rendered and extended in the networked world of distributed information to the user. Nine research objectives quantitatively and qualitatively characterize this direction:

1. Advance the technologies supporting federated repositories from the present state, in which independent repositories are federated using custom software, to a state in which generic software is commonly available and supports thousands of distributed, federated repositories.

2. Enlarge the effective collection capacity of a typical repository from thousands to millions of digital objects, including scalable indexing, cataloging, search, and retrieval.
3. Support digital objects as large as 100 megabytes and as small as 100 bytes.
4. Reduce response times for interaction with digital objects to sub-second levels, striving for a tenth of a second, where possible. High duplex bandwidth coupled with low response time provides the opportunity to explore new modes of interacting with information (broadband interoperability), in which the traditional query can be reconceived to include a much richer user and task context.
5. Expand the user's functional capabilities to interact with networked information, from the present play-and-display facilities of the Web to the correlate-and-manipulate requirements of a sophisticated information user engaged in network-based research and problem solving.
6. Raise the level of interoperability among users and information repositories from a high dependence on syntax, structure, and word choice, to a greater involvement of semantics, context, and concepts.
7. Extend search and filtering beyond bibliographic criteria to include contextual criteria relating to the task and the user.
8. Reduce language as a barrier to identifying and evaluating relevant information resources by providing translingual services for query and information extraction.
9. Advance the technology for general-purpose content extraction beyond forms and tagged document structures to include extraction of summary information (for example, topics) from semi-structured information sources.

This is the view from the late twentieth century, when the world began functioning in "Internet time." Just as old assumptions constrain new innovation, so can today's "realities" become constraining rather than liberating. *Caveat emptor.*

NOTES

1. Steve Lawrence and Lee Giles, "Accessibility of Information on the Web," *Nature* 400, no. 6740 (July 8, 1999): 107–109. For a summary of the study in *Nature,* see: http://wwwmetrics.com/

2. Michael Lesk, "How Much Information Is There in the World?" See: http://www.lesk.com/mlesk/ksg97/ksg.html

3. "The Uniform Computer Information Transactions Act (UCITA)," *EDUCAUSE*, March 2000. See: http://www.educause.edu/policy/ucita.html

4. Ronald L. Larsen, "Relaxing Assumptions . . . Stretching the Vision: A Modest View of Some Technical Issues," at http://www.dlib.org/dlib/april97/04larsen.html; and William Y. Arms, "Relaxing Assumptions about the Future of Digital Libraries: The Hare and the Tortoise," at http://www.dlib.org/dlib/april97/04arms.html

5. R. A. Freitas and W. P. Gilbreath, "Advanced Automation for Space Missions," National Technical Information Service N83-15348, 1980.

6. Peter Freeman and William Aspray, "The Supply of Information Technology Workers in the United States," Computing Research Association, May 1999. See: http://www.cra.org/reports/wits/cra.wits.html

7. "The Eighth Text REtrieval Conference (TREC 8)." See: http://trec.nist.gov/pubs/trec8/t8_proceedings.html

8. http://www.dlib.org

9. http://www.itl.nist.gov/iaui/894.02/related_projects/tipster/

10. Charles Wayne, "Topic Detection and Tracking (TDT) Overview and Perspective," 1998. See: http://www.itl.nist.gov/iaui/894.01/proc/darpa98/html/tdt10/tdt10.htm

11. Message Understanding Conference, Tipster Text Program. See: http://www.nlpir.nist.gov/related_projects/tipster/muc.htm

12. Summarization Evaluation Results, Tipster Text Program. See: http://www.nlpir.nist.gov/related_projects/tipster/sumslides.htm

13. Stuart K. Card, Jock Mackinlay, and Ben Shneiderman, *Readings in Information Visualization: Using Vision to Think* (San Francisco: Morgan Kaufmann, 1999).

14. SPIRE—Spatial Paradigm for Information Retrieval and Exploration, Battelle Pacific Northwest National Laboratory. See: http://multimedia.pnl.gov:2080/infoviz/spire/spire.html

15. Personal communication with Prof. Robert Frederking, Carnegie Mellon University.

16. http://www.darpa.mil/ito/research/tides/index.html

17. Paul Sommers, "Washington State Software Industry Workforce Challenges," Northwest Policy Center, Institute for Public Policy and Management, Graduate School of Public Affairs, University of Washington, October 20, 1998.

18. http://www.ncstrl.org

19. http://HTTP.CS.Berkeley.EDU/~wilensky/MVD.html

20. Andreas Paepcke et al., "Interoperability for Digital Libraries Worldwide," *Communications of the ACM* 41, no. 4 (April 1998): 33–42.

21. http://www.dli2.nsf.gov/eu_e.html#_Toc432270462

22. http://www.isi.edu/natural-language/projects/MuST.html

23. http://www-nlpir.nist.gov/related_projects/tipster/muc.htm

24. Proceedings of the DARPA Broadcast News Workshop, February 28–March 3, 1999, Hilton at Washington Dulles Airport, Herndon, Virginia, at: http://www.itl.nist.gov/iaui/894.01/proc/darpa99/. See also http://www.itl.nist.gov/iaui/894.01/proc/darpa98/html/tdt10/tdt10.htm

25. http://multimedia.pnl.gov:2080/topicography/

26. http://elib.cs.berkeley.edu/

27. http://www.canis.uiuc.edu/projects/interspace/

28. Joseph Alper, "Taming MEDLINE with Concept Spaces," *Science* 281, no. 5384 (September 18, 1998): 1785.

29. http://www.sims.berkeley.edu/research/metadata/

30. http://www.canis.uiuc.edu/interspace/

31. http://scils.rutgers.edu/baa9709/

32. http://www.canis.uiuc.edu/projects/interspace/

33. http://lobster.isi.edu/geoworldspubli/

3

Electronic Serials into the Millennium

FRIEDEMANN A. WEIGEL

To put our topic into the proper perspective, we need to step back in time and look at the history of the printed word. Think back to the time of Johannes Gutenberg, about 550 years ago. We all know that Gutenberg's contribution to publishing was *movable type*—which resulted in the ability to recycle the letters after a print run in order to print subsequent publications. What interests us about Gutenberg, however, is not his clever invention, but, rather, the fact that it succeeded. In economic terms, what was the point of an efficient mechanism for publishing the printed word in a world where practically nobody could read? Or in a world where practically nobody could afford to buy printed products? Nonetheless, Gutenberg's technology became a brilliant success. It took only about twenty years for the printing press to penetrate the market.

We live in Gutenberg times. Is there not a parallel between Gutenberg's "economically useless" technology and that of the electronic journal? Did we not supply the world with electronic information when most readers were barely getting started with e-mail, and the World Wide Web had not yet emerged? Or when most of our readers were technologically illiterate and, even if they were literate, preferred material that they could "read in

Originally presented as the keynote address at the Second Electronic Serials Institute, "Through the Arch: Electronic Serials from Acquisition to Access," April 24–25, 1998, St. Louis, Missouri.

45

the bathtub"? Did it not take far less than twenty years for electronic publications to penetrate the market through the World Wide Web?

There is a further parallel between movable type and online publishing. Five hundred fifty years ago, Gutenberg redefined the concept of a "page." His contribution was to dissolve the printed page into its smallest particles—letters—which could then be reformed and recycled as new words and new publications. Electronic publication similarly makes it possible to dissolve publications into atomic particles. The journal issue is no longer sacrosanct. The article itself is really the important unit, and if it is no longer tied to paper, there is no need to tie the article to an issue of a publication. We are no longer constrained by the print cycle, nor to the size limitations of a single issue. When information is ready to be published, it can be published. But publications can be atomized into even smaller units, such as title, abstract, references, and images, which can easily be reused for other purposes. Any one of these can stand alone and can easily be included in subsequent publications through hypertext links, so that even the concept of an "article" fades away.

HISTORY OF STM JOURNAL PUBLISHING

To understand the development of electronic journals, a brief overview of the history of journal publishing, specifically of scientific, technical, and medical (STM) journals, is in order.[1] The international STM journal market is geographically homogeneous, and the rules and economic mechanisms are fairly uniform throughout North America, Europe, Japan, Australia, and the Pacific Rim. In the 1970s, some publishers recognized the prevailing market dilemma that journal prices are not sensitive to the normal economic rules of supply and demand. They realized, for example, that there is no substitute for a given product and that the product has a limitless and basically free source of supply—scientists *must* publish (or perish). These publishers also understood that the product user (the researcher) is not the product buyer (the library), and, therefore, the user is not inspired to work toward controlling prices. These factors led to a quasi price-fixing situation. During the 1970s, major commercial STM publishers used a threefold strategy to increase their profits:

They imposed enormous price increases of 10 to 20 percent per year.

They reduced the discounts for agents.

They expanded their market share by taking over the publications of scholarly societies.

During this same period, libraries had sufficient budgets, and they were able to maintain a balance between the acquisitions budget and the published material to be acquired. In those years, agents supplied and supported "everything" that the libraries needed.

Then the 1980s emerged, and the earth began to tremble. The number of papers being published doubled, journal prices doubled, and library acquisitions budgets could not keep pace, growing by about 50 percent. The only hope of librarians was that upcoming technology would help solve the dilemma. Libraries reacted by:

Canceling journal subscriptions

Reducing the acquisition of books to support the serials habit

Reducing staff

Developing alternative strategies, such as document delivery and interlibrary loan

Focusing on optimizing work flows

Outsourcing processing wherever possible

Contracting directly with publishers for delivery of journals

Consolidating orders through only a few agents

Using the RFP/RFQ process for selecting agents

What was the effect on the subscription agents? A number of them were acquired or went out of business (Readmore, Majors, Kunst und Wissen, Faxon), and those that survived worked hard to optimize their work flows. They offered additional services. In cooperation with libraries, they began developing EDI links with library online systems. Some commercial publishers continued their pricing strategy for paper journals and began to play with electronic presentation and distribution of their journals. During the 1980s, some segments of the STM journal market developed into semimonopolies.

Enter the 1990s. The earthquake intensified. Libraries faced further budget cuts or received only modest increases. Commercial STM publishers continued their pricing policies with annual increases as large as 15 percent. Further concentration of the marketplace occurred. All market participants feared for the future. Disintermediation became a buzzword: a direct link between author and reader was suggested, a world without reviewing scientists, publishers, distributors, or libraries. STM publishers felt the need to go electronic, and the first serious electronic solutions tested the market.

THE DEVELOPMENT OF E-JOURNALS

The earliest full-text electronic journals were distributed in the 1980s on CD-ROM for use within the library. In the late 1980s, the first online e-journals were distributed by e-mail, using electronic discussion list technology. Then came gopher distribution, which was quickly supplanted by the World Wide Web. Some milestones include:

1987 *New Horizons in Adult Education,* the first peer-reviewed journal distributed on the Internet

1990 *Postmodern Culture,* a very well-known early, peer-reviewed journal distributed on the Internet

1992 *Online Journal of Current Clinical Trials,* from OCLC, the first peer-reviewed online journal to contain graphics

1991–1995 The TULIP project, representing the entry of commercial publishers into online publishing. In this project, Elsevier distributed the electronic version of print journals to several academic institutions, which mounted them on their own networks

1993 JSTOR, the first major project to convert back files of print journals to electronic form

1993–1994 The World Wide Web took the academic world by storm

1995 HighWire Press, the Internet imprint of Stanford University

To see how far we have come, it is interesting, almost amusing, to examine some quotes from the early days of e-journal publication:

PMC [*Postmodern Culture*] comes out three times a year . . . and is free to the public and to libraries via electronic mail. . . . The journal is also available on computer diskette and microfiche; it is distributed in a variety of diskette formats . . . but no issue will exceed 720 KB of data, the equivalent of one 3.5" or two 5.25" low-density diskettes.[2]

Today, there are some thirty networked electronic journals, of which about eight are refereed or lightly refereed, and there are probably at least sixty networked electronic newsletters.[3]

E-Journals are remarkable because:

They can be delivered to the desktop (although the desktop needs a computer!).

They can be read by more than one person at a time.

The text can be searched.

They can include multimedia and graphics, in color, at marginal cost.

They can be published more quickly than paper publications.

They can be interactive; that is, they can foster an online exchange of ideas by e-mail.

If they are on the Web, they can take advantage of the ability to make hyperlinks, both internally and to other publications. Thus, readers can link directly to references cited in an article and also, with additional effort on the part of publishers and indexers, to later articles that cite the article being read.

Articles can be retrieved directly through links from abstracting and indexing databases.

The content can be reproduced, forwarded, or modified (leading to possible problems with copyright protection and the preservation of authenticity).

They allow readers to apply the power of computers and the Internet to their reading process.

The main disadvantage, in addition to the potential copyright and authenticity problems, is that, unless they are also printed on paper, e-journals require specialized equipment for reading.

ISSUES INVOLVING E-JOURNALS

Issues involving e-journals need to be examined from several perspectives: those of the publisher, the agent, the library, the author or researcher, and the reader. Two important threads will carry through the entire discussion. First, business and legal issues are far more important than technical ones, because technical solutions that do not address economics and intellectual property rights are bound to fail. Second, the Internet has globalized the activities of researching, writing, publishing, distributing, and acquiring information and has overcome the barriers of geography and time. The Internet itself might become the lab, the publishing house, the agency, and the library.

Publisher Issues

Publishers face a number of challenges. How can they take advantage of the fact that they are no longer tied to the print publication cycle? Material can be published more quickly; in fact, articles can come out as soon as they are written, without waiting for the next "issue." Will the concept of volume and issue disappear? When you get right down to it, how should a journal/serial be defined in today's electronic environment? Is a real-time news feed the same thing as a newspaper? Is the occasional online distribution of announcements to a society the same thing as a newsletter? How can publishers take advantage of the possibilities of interactivity? Letters to the editor can take place instantaneously, leading to online discussions that can be linked to the articles to which they refer.

The real concerns of the publishers, however, are far more down to earth. How can they maintain or improve their income stream? How can they broaden the distribution of their journal? How can they increase their membership? How can they achieve a stronger position compared to the competition? Sometimes the question is even more basic: Will the organization or the journal survive?

A standard business maxim says that the only sure thing about a business plan is that it will prove to be wrong. Several years ago the publishers of the *Journal of Biological Chemistry* felt they had reached the limits of physical information distribution with their weekly printed issue. A single print issue with about nine hundred pages had simply become too heavy to allow for reasonable transport, usage, and storage; one issue of *JBC* weighs about four pounds. The publishers felt that going online would be instrumental in lowering the subscription price by about 20 percent, which should have been a great incentive for readers to switch from the print to the online version. *JBC* went online with the goal of totally replacing the print medium with electronic delivery. What happened? The number of articles submitted rose sharply, and the number of *print* subscriptions went *up*. So much for the plan.

Agent Issues

A persistent rumor is floating about that the days of the subscription agent are over. Squeezed between the libraries looking for lower prices and the publishers raising their prices, agents seem to have become the victims of disintermediation. This unfounded rumor is based on two misperceptions:

1. The market is a "linear flow" of goods (information) and money between producer (publisher) and consumer (library or even reader). We know that we now work in a networked setting where new services and partnerships grow continually. In a network, each unit is an intermediary.
2. The agent no longer has any added value to offer. In an article in *The Bookseller*, Christopher Gasson mentions that Jim Rose of Blackwell "is confident that the advance of electronic distribution technology will actually enhance the value that subscription agents provide to their customers. He believes that the agent's

main role is in creating simplicity out of chaos, and electronic systems are creating a lot more chaos to simplify."[4]

This leads us back to the two leitmotivs of globalization and the underestimation of business issues. Globalization is an issue only for those companies that in the past adhered to the principle of supplying materials based on the country or continent of origin. In the world of the wide Web, country of origin no longer makes any sense. E-journals permit and require global distribution.

Most agents have also suffered from underestimating the importance of business issues with regard to e-journals. Basically, all the major subscription agencies responded to the "threat" of e-journals with a hasty technical answer: agency-based aggregation systems. This solution is anxiety-driven and based on the premise that controlling access will boost sales. If a customer is locked into an aggregated system, then that customer will have to continue to purchase e-journals from the aggregator rather than subject its users to a confusing array of user interfaces. The aggregation solution overlooks the fact that libraries already have two excellent means of aggregating their journal collections: their own library catalogs and the subject-based abstracting and indexing services. Users are not well served by aggregations of electronic journal articles that happen to be provided by one vendor; what they need is a comprehensive index to all the articles in a specific subject area, both electronic and paper.

The most valuable service agencies can deliver is related to acquisitions rather than to direct delivery to the user. After so many years of a fairly simple and widely accepted business model for journal delivery, e-journals have caused acquisitions to become more difficult again, opening up a wide field for agency activities.

Library Issues

Licensing, Pricing, and Access Control

Licensing, pricing, and access control issues are bound firmly together because the price and access restrictions are—or should be—included in the license agreement. The very concept of a license to a journal is new. When libraries bought printed journals, they paid their money and received the paper issues, which they then owned and archived, bound, sent out on interlibrary loan, or placed on reserve, and from which single articles could be photocopied for single users, in accordance with fair use copyright law.

Now suddenly we're talking about "licenses" to content. What does that mean? There is no single clear and handy definition, but it does seem to mean "permission to use (that is, to read) the information, and maybe print it for individual use," as in the print world. The problems arise because it is so easy to access digital information from remote locations and to replicate and redistribute it.

A fine place to learn about current thinking on e-journal licensing is on the Liblicense Web site, hosted by Yale University.[5] There one may find sample licenses and valuable advice, which may be summarized as: "Don't agree to do anything you're not prepared to do," and "There is nearly always space for negotiation." The "authorized use" sample clauses from the Liblicense Web site list the most important licensing questions that should be asked:

Who can get access to the information?

Where can they do it?

How long can they do it?

What can they do with it?

For what purposes may they use it? Electronic reserves?
    Interlibrary loan? Course packs?

The number of variations on the pricing of Internet-accessible e-journals is practically infinite and can be based on several factors: whether or not paper (or CD-ROM) is received; whether the subscription is based on an individual, an institutional, or a membership arrangement, carrying on a paper-based tradition; the number of e-journals subscribed to from the same vendor (volume discount); the length of subscription (cheaper for a longer term); consortial pricing; site licensing (flat rate for an entire institution, based on size of institution, number of simultaneous users, or number of transactions); pay-per-view for single articles; charter memberships (for example, JSTOR); age of material available (backfiles are usually cheaper than current issues); and whether authors are charged a fee to publish.

Standards

The impact of the World Wide Web on e-journals cannot be overstated! Contrary to popular understanding, electronic journals existed before the Web, but there was very little standardization among them. Most were distributed on CD-ROM, and, generally, each required its own viewing software. Others were distributed as ASCII text in the form of e-mail messages. The early formatted (more than ASCII) e-journals distributed on the Internet required a specialized client for viewing. This was a nuisance, because the clients had to be distributed and installed on the desktop before users could read the e-journals.

The World Wide Web has become the de facto standard for the delivery of e-journals. That is, we expect that readers will have an Internet connection and a World Wide Web browser available, and users expect to be able to find what they want on the Web without using specialized clients. These assumptions, however, raise some problems, and not just questions of bandwidth.

In addition to official networking standards, such as TCP/IP, http, and ftp, we find three more groups of standards used on the World Wide Web: delivery formats, identifiers, and descriptors.

Delivery Formats For the delivery of pages there are several choices, the most popular of which are HTML and PDF. HTML is an IETF (Internet Engineering Task Force) standard and is nice because it is platform-independent; that is, it can be read and displayed on any computer that has a browser. As ASCII text, it transmits relatively quickly, and it can be indexed and searched easily. The downside is that one never *really* knows what a page will look like on a specific browser because this depends on screen size, settings, and so on. More important, it is easy for a malicious user to copy, modify, and retransmit a page of ASCII text, leaving no evidence whatsoever that this has happened.

To preserve the look and integrity of the page, it is safer to use page images. It would be possible, of course, to transmit pages as bit-mapped images (JPEG or GIF), but they take a long time to transmit, don't print so well, and are more difficult to index. The most frequently used alternative to HTML is PDF, Adobe's image capture method. It too has become a de facto standard, largely because Adobe distributes it free of charge. The user does need to load the viewing application, but getting it from the World Wide Web is easy enough. The main attraction of PDF for e-journals is that it produces a page that looks exactly like the printed page, including the page numbers. It also produces an extremely refined printout. An added feature is that the text portions can be transmitted, and indexed, as ASCII text. Other page-delivery mechanisms, such as CatchWord's RealPage and IBM's TechExplorer, are also being used, but they do not have the market share that PDF has achieved.

Identifiers Another area in which standards are important is that of identifiers. In the library world, standardized identifiers, including ISBN, ISSN, LCCN, and call number, have been used for many years. Identifying individual items, such as journal issues or specific articles, has proved to be somewhat more difficult, but the identifier could still be linked to a physical piece. With e-journals, identifying items becomes problematic, because items are no longer physically tied together—bound, as it were. Individual journal articles need to be identified as "digital objects." In fact, an article itself may consist of a number of digital objects, or, rather, a web of objects, including one or more text pieces, graphics, links, and other multimedia pieces.

With distributed electronic information on the Web, the location of the object must also be identified. So far, URLs have been used for this purpose. URLs can change, so what is needed are schemes for persistent pointers to the objects. OCLC's PURL and Corporation for National Research Initiatives' (CNRI) Handle are reasonable solutions to this problem, but they are nowhere near being universally adopted. The publishing industry has proposed additional uses for identifiers—rights management and billing—in the DOI, or Digital Object Identifier. Is this perhaps loading too much responsibility onto a single identifier?

Descriptors   Finally, we should talk about descriptive standards, in particular, metadata. The W3 Consortium in its press release for RDF, the Resource Description Framework, suggests the following uses for metadata:[6]

  resource discovery (that is, searching)

  description, to uniquely describe an object

  relationships, to allow intelligent software agents to facilitate knowledge sharing and exchange

  content rating for child protection and privacy protection

  grouping collections of objects that represent a single logical "document"

  describing intellectual property rights of online documents

As we can see, the function of metadata goes well beyond what we expected from the online catalog, which was designed for discovery and description.

Acquisition and Distribution

Is life any easier for librarians? Not at all. How can one find a balance, with one foot in the futuristic world of e-journals, while the other must remain firmly planted in the old world of print material? NELINET's Ann Devenish, in announcing the 1998 conference "Digital Reality: Managing Electronic Resources," pointed out that the decision to acquire an electronic journal means much more than to "make room for it on the shelves."[7] The acquisition has an impact on every aspect of the library, and she listed the following nine questions that should be resolved:

1. Who makes the acquisition decision?
2. Who negotiates the contract?

3. Is the technology in place for local or remote access?
4. Whose departmental budget funds it?
5. Do the staff members involved have the required skills?
6. How are storage and preservation resolved?
7. Is there access from the library catalog?
8. Is the e-journal union-listed?
9. What are the copyright implications for ILL and
   the reserve room?

Let us look at some examples of the ways in which electronic information distribution has changed the library and, indeed, the entire academic landscape. Chuck Hamaker asked whether too much user information—meaning information *about* users—is available already. He was concerned that with the introduction of e-journals, one of the protections that libraries traditionally provide, anonymity, is in jeopardy. "How much of a right does a department head on campus have to know what information faculty and grad students in the departments are using? . . . Is privacy a part of our responsibilities, as much as price and connectivity and content?"[8] Hamaker also asked "when is a journal not a journal?" and writes that he:

> first began to realize how *not* full text . . . many titles could be when I was looking for an article on Mormonism. I could not pull it up with keyword searching . . . the problem was some spell checking where the article was keyed had turned every instance of "Mormon" into "moron." So the word did not appear in the title, text, body, etc. How unreliable "aggregator" full text could be became immediately apparent.[9]

This is a somewhat brutal example of the lack of quality control found in some aggregator systems. Do we really find and get what we are supposed to get? Does my screen show me a complete and correct picture of the original source?

On March 25, 1998, the International Coalition of Library Consortia (ICOLC) released its "Statement of Current Perspective and Preferred Practices for the Selection and Purchase of Electronic Information."[10] ICOLC claims to have established for the first time an international perspective on consortial licensing and purchasing of electronic information by libraries. The statement calls for the development of multiple pricing models, separating charges for electronic licenses from those for paper subscriptions and lowering the cost for the electronic information below that for print subscriptions. This document also illustrates to some degree the polarization that is taking place between publishers and libraries, putting them into conflicting positions, rather than identifying the problems and suggesting adequate resolutions.

Researcher or Author Issues

At the root of the researcher's needs is the requirement to be published in a peer-reviewed journal, partly in order to secure tenure, promotion, and reputation, but also as a means for sharing knowledge and discovery. The rising cost of research publication and, simultaneously, the increasing demand for it, has led to calls for reform in the tenure and promotion process and changes in publication procedures. Electronic publishing plays an important role in this debate, presumably because it can be done more quickly and cheaply than traditional print publication, and also because it promotes a much greater degree of interactivity.

On March 31, 1998, the Association of Research Libraries, together with the Association of American Universities and the Pew Higher Education Roundtable, announced the publication of a remarkable report, "To Publish and Perish," which states: "To achieve progress on any initiative entails a willingness to recast how research results are communicated and the means by which the producers of those results are evaluated."[11] The report suggests that universities consider the following far-reaching actions:

> End the preoccupation with numbers: Faculty committees should make clear that quality of work counts for more than the sheer number of publications.
>
> Be smart shoppers: Rethink journal subscriptions, concentrating on the most highly read journals and using cooperative resource sharing purchases for the rest.
>
> Get a handle on property rights.
>
> Invest in electronic forms of scholarly communication.
>
> Decouple publication and faculty evaluation for the purposes of promotion and tenure.

Reader Issues

Let us raise one overarching question: *What do users need?* First, users need author, title, and subject access to the journal *articles*. This means the ability to search a comprehensive collection of *all* articles in a particular discipline, not just those published by a particular publisher. The mechanism is already in place, and it comes from the abstracting and indexing (A&I) services. These are the bibliographic databases. What is still missing in most cases is the link from the citation to the full text of the articles, and this is where energies are now being concentrated. Do we really want full-text searching of journal articles? Probably, but not as a replacement for intelligent subject searching.

Second, users need subject and title access to the journal *titles* themselves. Users should be able to find a specific title by searching the library's online catalog. The holdings statement should make clear which titles and which issues are available electronically, and users should be able to link from the catalog directly to the online journal. If multiple versions are available, all should be cataloged, so the user can access the one that best serves his or her needs. There is nothing new under the sun in this scenario. Users find articles just as they always have, through bibliographic databases. They find titles just as they always have, through the online catalog. Only the delivery of the text has been improved.

Third, users need access to back issues, raising an extremely important issue for electronic publications: *archiving and preservation*. An anecdote from the Stanford University Libraries may help put the question of preservation of electronic resources into perspective. During the rainstorms of the winter of 1998, the ground floors of three libraries were flooded. Approximately 70,000 books were damaged along with great quantities of microfiche and personal computers. A little more than 80 percent of the books were saved, all the microfiche were lost, and all the data on the computer hard disks were recovered.

Why are we so concerned with preservation of electronic data? Because there are more aspects to be concerned with than there were with paper. Preservation of electronic information has several aspects:

- *Reliability of the media.* With paper, this was our only concern, and because we have had centuries of experience, we know what to expect. We don't have this kind of experience with digital media, and we don't know how long it will last. The approach taken by most institutions is to "refresh" the data; that is, copy it periodically to be sure that it can still be read. Another problem is that most digital media (tapes and disks, but not CD-ROMs) can be overwritten accidentally.

- *Readability of the media.* If the media need special equipment to be read, it is essential to migrate the data to new media before the old equipment becomes obsolete. (We should note here that it has become almost a cliché to proclaim that "electronic information will never replace paper." Fortunately, we are hearing less and less about how one can't curl up in bed with an e-journal or read it in the bathtub or on the train—although laptops make it pretty easy on the train these days! There seems to be fairly universal agreement that, though paper is not obsolete, electronic resources are here to stay.)

- *Data format.* Different data formats may need specialized software in order to be read. That can get expensive if everybody has to keep all the software available. It would be better to use a platform-independent format, such as XML.

- *Authenticity and integrity of the source.* It is very easy to modify digital data; therefore, the archiving facility needs not only a mechanism to ensure that the data preserved are identical to the data produced, but also a way to prove it.

A further point is that, if the full capabilities of e-journals are used, it will be impossible to archive them on paper. Dynamic data, such as hotlinks on Web pages, are difficult to store on paper. So are embedded movies, programs, sounds, and data files. Paper backup is not the solution.

In one respect, however, digital information is much easier to preserve than paper was. One good copy can be duplicated indefinitely with practically no effort. All this leads to the big question: Who should be responsible for maintaining the archive of our electronic journals? Publishers? Libraries? Consortia? Scholarly societies? A national or international archive? The real problem is that we are not organized for electronic archiving. Policies have not been developed, we don't have standards for measuring deterioration, and technology is changing too fast for comfort. The sooner we face the fact that change is the only constant, the sooner we will face the problems. They won't be resolved by waiting.

MULTIMEDIA: THE NEXT STEP FOR E-JOURNALS?

In German, another word for *verstehen* (to understand) is *begreifen,* which probably translates best as "to grasp" or "to catch on." Linguistically, this is telling, and implies that the processes of learning and understanding can include senses other than sight alone—in this case, touch. When one considers the things one remembers best, were they first sensed through sight or hearing, or perhaps through taste or touch or smell? It is clear that multimedia technologies have the potential to revolutionize learning and teaching. It is an interesting exercise to consider the various senses, how we can "publish" for each of them, how they can be included in print versus electronic publications, and which are transmitted best by paper and which electronically.

> *Sight:* text, images, moving images, and holograms. Of these, all can be represented quite nicely on paper except moving images, and, to some extent, holograms. All are easily transmitted electronically, including holograms.

> *Sound:* Like moving images, sound exists through time, so it can't be transported by means of paper. But it's not too hard to distribute sound recordings accompanying a paper issue.

Touch: Touch-sensitive technology is beginning to appear, but we're still a long way from making it available at the average desktop.

Smell: Ironically, advertisers have been inserting scented leaflets into printed magazines for a long time, but no one has even thought of transmitting aromas over the Internet.

Taste: Tastes have appeared neither on paper (probably for hygienic reasons more than because it can't be done) nor over the Internet, but because taste is chemical, it faces the same delivery problems as aroma.

And, of course, virtual reality consists of stimulating all the senses together.

What does all this have to do with e-journals? Simply put, you can transmit more sensory-related data electronically than on paper. James Wallis, then at IBM's Watson Labs, stated at a Top Management Roundtable of the Society for Scholarly Publishing: "The problem with you publishers is you think you add value. Well, you don't. You force me to reduce the information in my scientific papers so that [it] will fit on a flat printed page."[12]

The online journal *Earth Interactions,* which began publication in January 1997, is overcoming these limitations.[13] This geophysical journal presents such nonprint information as dynamic visualizations of data, rotatable 3-D images, animations of numerical simulations over time, computer code (programs), virtual reality displays, and small datasets.

CONCLUSION

We can't hide our heads in the sand. E-journals are not a novelty; they are here to stay. Let us embrace them by looking at our environment for existing tools, procedures, and services and determine which have been most worthwhile in the past and how we can use them in the future. The OPAC, the A&I services, the subscription vendors—all are still relevant and essential to our effective use of e-journals.

Let us not look at e-journals solely as a technical issue. Technical issues are easy to solve. We will really use the new media to their best extent only if we come to grips with the legal and business issues. These must be solved by all the involved parties together: authors, publishers, researchers, readers, libraries. We are fortunate to live in Gutenberg times. We have the chance to influence future reading, learning, and teaching, and it is a wonderful challenge.

NOTES

1. A synopsis of the trends in the journal publishing community during the last three decades of the twentieth century and librarians' reactions to those developments may be found in: "Trends in Scientific Scholarly Journal Publishing in the United States," by Carol Tenopir and Donald W. King in *Journal of Scholarly Publishing* 28, no. 3 (April 1997): 135–170 and in "The Changing Economic Model of Scholarly Publishing: Uncertainty, Complexity, and Multimedia Serials" by John Cox in *Library Acquisitions* 22, no. 2 (summer 1998): 161–166.

2. Eyal Amiran and John Unsworth, "Postmodern Culture: Publishing in the Electronic Medium." *Public-Access Computer Systems Review* 2, no.1 (1991): 6. See also: http://info.lib.uh.edu/pr/v2/n1/amiran.2n1

3. Ann Okerson, "The Electronic Journal: What, Whence, and When?" *Public-Access Computer Systems Review* 2, no. 1 (1991): 10. See also: http://info.lib.uh. edu/pr/v2/n1/okerson.2n1 and http://www.library.yale.edu/~okerson/pacs. html

4. Christopher Gasson, "An End to Intermediaries?" *Bookseller,* no. 4806 (January 30, 1998): 24.

5. See: http://www.library.yale.edu/~llicense/index/shtml

6. See: http://www.w3.org/Press/RDF

7. Conference announcement, n.d. For the archives of the conference, see: http://www.nelinet.net/conf/digital/dig_real.htm

8. *Newsletter on Serials Pricing Issues,* no. 205 (March 18, 1998). See: http://www.lib.unc.edu/prices/1998/PRIC205.HTML

9. March 19, 1998. See: http://www.library.yale.edu/~llicense/ListArchives?9803/msg00045.html

10. See: http://www.library.yale.edu/consortia/statement.html

11. "To Publish and Perish," *Policy Perspectives,* special issue, 7, no. 4 (March 1998). See: http://www.arl.org/scomm/pew/pewrept.html)

12. Judy Holoviak and Keith L. Seitter, "Transcending the Limitations of the Printed Page," *Journal of Electronic Publishing* 3, no. 1 (September 1997). See: http://www.press.umich.edu/jep/03-01/EI.html

13. See: http://earthinteractions.org/

4

Managing Electronic Serials

An Overview

SHARON CLINE MCKAY

ELECTRONIC ISN'T CHEAPER

In the early days of e-journals, many people seemed to have the impression that it was cheaper to produce journals in electronic form, so the e-versions should be priced lower than the print versions. Such people assumed that the costs of paper, printing, binding, and distribution would be saved, and, therefore, electronic publishing should be less costly. Some scholarly publishers actually offered their e-journals at a lower subscription price, for example, 90 percent of the print price. However, publishers' costs still include several fixed expenses regardless of the format, for such activities as editorial work and peer review. To produce an e-version, publishers must fund research and development for an electronic delivery mechanism and conversion of the data from the printable files to a format that can be viewed on the Web. They must continue to support both formats, because all customers don't immediately cancel their print subscription in favor of the electronic. Additional hardware is frequently needed to produce electronic files and support online access to them.

Based on presentations at the Second Electronic Serials Institute, "Through the Arch: Electronic Serials from Acquisition to Access," April 24–25, 1998, St. Louis, Missouri, and the Third Electronic Serials Institute, "Blazing the Trail: Electronic Serials from Acquisition to Access," April 16–17, 1999, Portland, Oregon.

Costs to deliver e-journals are also significant for the aggregator. This new breed of information agent has arisen to fill a need so that users are able to gain access to publications from multiple publishers in one system with a single user interface. Aggregators can be subscription agents, abstract and index (A&I) producers (secondary publishers), primary publishers acting as agents for other publishers, or other types of information providers. These companies must forge new relationships to create the necessary delivery mechanisms for access to electronic journals. Traditional subscription agencies that handle other serials-related matters are moving into the new role of delivering access to e-journals through systems designed to collect and index search terms for journal articles from multiple publishers. The cost of these systems includes linking systems, both internal and external, as well as internal handling operations. No longer is service just a matter of sending an order to the publisher on behalf of a client, handling claims if needed, and producing related reports. Aggregators must establish links to publishers' URLs down to the journal article level and maintain those links whenever a server is moved or the link is otherwise broken.

Even libraries bear extra costs associated with setting up and maintaining e-journal access. The first thing that costs libraries more, in the form of extra staff time, is to negotiate and obtain licenses. This activity can be very time-consuming and presents a great challenge for anyone who has little or no experience with legal documents. Expert counsel may be required, with the possibility of incurring additional costs if legal staff is not readily available within the organization. Library staff must register IP (Internet Protocol) addresses and domain names with each publisher or aggregator used, and then track which journals are available through which IP addresses, if different. Staff must also create and maintain URL links from the library's catalog or Web site to give users access to the content of the e-journals. Publicity is necessary to let library users know what is available and how to get access. Very likely there will be an impact on many different budgets because of additional costs for e-journals, over and above the subscription price for the print versions, and libraries must decide whether to maintain the print subscriptions if there are added charges for the e-version. A pay-per-view option that allows access to peripheral publications not on subscription may also be a solution, and, in some cases, may be more cost effective.

PRICING MODELS

A wide variety of pricing models are offered to libraries. Package deals for consortia have been quite popular, but they typically offer an all-or-nothing situation. In that case, if all libraries in a consortium pay for access to all the publications of a particular publisher, the price per journal is low. However, those libraries that use only a few of the journals end up subsidizing those who use many or all of them. Some aggregators offer a pick-and-choose option to enable individual customers to subscribe only to a select number of journals while providing a common user interface with the ability to search across all publishers and all journals. A pay-per-view option is currently offered by about ten scholarly publishers, presenting users with the capability of getting an article from a journal not on subscription. The question is: Who pays? If organizational funds are used, who is given this privilege and who does without? If the individual is required to use his or her own funds, questions about fairness and equal access for the "have-nots" are raised.

NEW ECONOMIC MODELS

Publishers have been comfortable with the print subscription model for many years and are likely to continue to offer that model as one option, if not the only one. Transaction purchases provide unpredictable revenue. Is this additional revenue over and above the subscription base, or does it replace institutional subscriptions? We may be moving toward a just-in-time or just-for-you environment instead of the just-in-case situation of the past. Libraries have purchased journals based on collection-development assessments of the needs of their primary users. If articles are simply retrieved from any journal based on user requests, does this affect collection development, and what sort of picture of users' needs is being formed?

Another economic model beginning to emerge is that of a package for a specific number of articles. For example, the library indicates that it wishes to purchase one hundred articles during the year from among the journals produced by a particular publisher. Users then determine which articles they want from which journals. This model may require less or even no involvement on the part of collection-development professionals. It is also less likely to result in a cohesive collection of materials because the material is being requested by individuals for their personal use, not for the collection in general.

ARCHIVES

The topic of archiving has generated endless debate. Archives are themselves storehouses, whether maintained by the publisher, an agent, or the library itself. "Perpetual access" is the ability to continue to retrieve articles from the storehouse maintained by the publisher or a designated agent, and raises many questions. Who should maintain the archives? Who should pay to support the archives and continued access? What kind of data refreshment will be needed in the future to continue to allow access to older data when technology changes? Should libraries that have cancelled their subscriptions still be allowed to access older materials for which they paid? Exactly what should be archived, and for how long? Should every publication in every discipline be archived, or only those publications that are deemed worthwhile for the long term? How does one define "long term," and does the definition depend on the discipline? Who has the power to decide what is worthy of being archived and what not?

At the root of this debate is the issue of ownership versus access. When a print journal is purchased, the issues become the physical property of the subscriber. Whether the issues are circulated or maintained in closed stacks, bound or left unbound, mutilated or stolen or protected from abuse, they are nonetheless under the control of the purchaser who can give users continued access for as long as desired. Environmental concerns and space requirements are the responsibility of the purchaser, who owns the journals. Any expenses incurred in housing, maintaining, and preserving the printed materials are also the purchaser's responsibility. If desired, printed journals may be removed from the collection; they can be offered to another library or discarded. If issues are found to be missing or damaged, usually they can be replaced by a photocopy from another library, if they are no longer available from the publisher.

When an organization subscribes to an e-journal, however, it is paying for access, not ownership, which is vastly different. An online journal does not reside within the purchaser's control. The files are usually held by the publisher or an appointed agent at a remote site. If the publisher ceases to publish the title, goes out of business, or otherwise stops making the electronic file available, the subscriber can do little to gain access. Under licensing agreements, the subscriber is usually not allowed to download and store the complete run of a journal as an electronic file.

AGENT SERVICES

Libraries generally prefer to use subscription agents rather than ordering directly from publishers. Using an agent reduces staff workload and minimizes the number of invoices to be processed through an institution's accounting department. Other than placing orders, agents also provide the following services for libraries requiring e-journals:

Obtaining and reviewing
licenses

Registration

Subscription validation

User authentication

Usage statistics

Setting up and maintaining
URL links and ensuring
secure links to publishers

Networking advice

Publicity materials

Availability reports

Collection development

Budgeting

Combined invoices

Online claiming

Dispatch information

Single point of support

User Preferences

User preferences and habits should be considered when choosing a gateway or an aggregator service. Users don't usually search by publisher, so it is important to provide a service that covers multiple publishers. Users also frequently want cross-publisher or cross-discipline access, although some users would prefer a service that focuses on their primary discipline. They want capabilities of searching and browsing, and many take advantage of alerting services to know when new issues of favorite journals have been released, or when an article from any journal addresses a topic of interest. Some services provide these alerting features for each user independently, or for groups of users wishing to be alerted about the same journal issues or articles.

Some users find it advantageous to be able to access citations and abstracts, even if their institution has no subscription to the journals themselves. Others prefer not to be tempted by knowing about articles that cannot easily be accessed. If the electronic version of an article isn't available, it may be accessible in the library's print collection, or it may be available by fax or e-mail delivery. Most users who access articles electronically print them out for later reading. Electronic access simply means articles of interest can be retrieved from the desktop or laptop anytime from anywhere.

TECHNOLOGICAL CONSIDERATIONS

Changing technology must be considered because formats and both hardware and software are not static. Storage is becoming cheaper, and capacities are growing enormously. It is relatively inexpensive to store lots of data for a long time, especially if the data are stored in a compressed state. However, access to that data can present a problem as methods of compression change and retrieval methods improve.

Formats

Some systems deliver multiple formats, including PDF and RealPage, which can now be viewed using the free Acrobat reader from Adobe. Some also provide access to articles in ASCII text without graphics or illustrations. Although an argument may be made that these are not true electronic journals, having access to them does expand the number of journals available by electronic means as opposed to needing to retrieve them physically.

Access Points

Libraries can easily provide access to e-journals from the online catalog by putting the appropriate URL in the 856 tag of the MARC record. The library Web site is another popular point of access. In both cases, maintenance is the responsibility of the library or computer center staff, and it should be noted that the frequency with which publishers' servers change can create a significant workload. Many users want to be able to access e-journal articles through links from abstracting and indexing databases. These are being created by several A&I publishers in partnership with aggregators and service providers. In addition, Z39.50 protocols are implemented by some systems as a way of using a single user interface to access a library's catalog, plus the catalogs of other libraries and databases with dissimilar interfaces. Most users, however, rely on the common technology provided by standard Web browsers available commercially.

CONCLUSION

Electronic information is attractive but expensive. Different management techniques are required to deal with e-journals, and they may be handled by staff separate from those who deal with print subscriptions. Libraries need extra funds to pay for e-journals to avoid having to cancel print subscriptions. If possible, library staff should try to allocate money in a separate budget earmarked for experimentation. If the experiment proves valid, then long-term funding must be sought to cover continued access. We live in a world of rapid and tremendous change. Our responses to that change must be strategic, and we must seek out partners to help us deal with the challenges. Partnerships are needed among all the players in the information industry—publishers (both primary and secondary), agents, and librarians—in order to resolve the issues.

5

Management and Technical Considerations for Acquiring and Accessing Electronic Serials

GEORGE MACHOVEC

Most libraries have embraced the need to move forward into the digital age. In addition to offering access to their integrated library systems over the Internet, libraries are aggressively offering access to abstracting and indexing services, electronic journals, materials from their own digitization efforts, and many other kinds of information. This paradigm shift in libraries from print to electronic access to information has taken over two decades . . . and much more is still to happen. To cope most effectively with these changes and move into the new millennium, however, libraries must contend with a variety of management issues. This chapter will review the technical concerns libraries face and examine some options for integrating electronic resources into the collection.

MANAGEMENT CHALLENGES

The Internet is crucial to virtually everything libraries do. With the exception of a few leased lines that libraries may use for enterprise-critical applications (for example, some libraries have leased lines to OCLC for guaranteed bandwidth for cataloging or database access), virtually all

Based on presentations at the Second Electronic Serials Institute, "Through the Arch: Electronic Serials from Acquisition to Access," April 24–25, 1998, St. Louis, Missouri, and the Third Electronic Serials Institute, "Blazing the Trail: Electronic Serials from Acquisition to Access," April 16–17, 1999, Portland, Oregon.

access to electronic resources is through the public Internet. More than ever, libraries need to be involved with such issues as bandwidth availability, who the local Internet Service Provider (ISP) is, wiring within the library and institution, and how "close" the library is to major electronic resources from a networking perspective. To ensure that their needs are being met, libraries must become involved with the networking/telecommunications and computing arms of their parent organization. A passive approach to Internet access could be a major mistake, as many outside the library community have no clue about the paradigm shifts taking place in the information industry and about what libraries actually need.

Partnerships

With the vast array of electronic resources and projects at the regional and national levels, it is key for libraries to develop strategic partnerships. When does a library use various electronic databases and tools? With which projects does a library become involved? Because of the limited availability of funds and human resources, many projects are best done not at the institutional level, but by linking with other initiatives at the local, regional, or national levels.

One of the biggest mistakes a library can make is to launch projects that are duplicative of efforts being made by others. Often, duplicative projects occur because of ignorance—not knowing what is happening within the regional or national community—or because of pride or a competitive spirit. It is far better to focus on unique initiatives that add to the overall improvement of services. Libraries must choose their partnerships carefully, be sure to be involved in wider efforts, and keep informed about developments in the marketplace and in the library community.

Consider who the library's natural partners or vendors for different tasks might be. Are there organizations outside the traditional library world that should be considered, such as private companies, museums, historical societies, governmental agencies, or schools? Efforts need to be carefully coordinated to maximize limited local resources.

Legal, Political, and Economic Considerations

Most challenges to new electronic initiatives are not technical but legal, political, or economic. On the legal front, libraries must deal with intellectual property issues, copyright, licensing provisions, and contract interpretation as well as the reality of how these relate to practice. Politics can occur within a library, between libraries, and between other competing organizations. Poor management of the politics can slow, cripple, or even kill the best of projects. Economic challenges are crucial because most libraries are underfunded. Looking for new sources of revenue outside traditional funding mechanisms will make the difference between a good library and a great library.

Standards

Standards are critical to virtually everything that is done. Most systems are built around arrays of standards or "best practices" guidelines. Departure from national standards is usually not advised and may cause unexpected problems later. Even if certain national standards are not the best, getting involved, working within the standard, and attempting to change the standard at the national level work best. Whenever possible, libraries should acquire software and data sets that employ national standards, and data should be created in compliance with national standards as well. RFPs and RFQs should require compliance with standards as far as is practical, and libraries should get involved in partnerships that build standards-compliant solutions.

Remote Users

Remote or distance users should receive the same level of service as on-site users. In the academic world, this is true for distance education classes as well as for students, faculty, or staff who are not on campus but may be working at home, in the office, or in any location around the world. Libraries must pay attention to remote user authentication for all electronic resources. It should be unnecessary for patrons to come to a physical building or campus in order to access an electronic resource that is distributed over the network. Access should be possible anywhere at any time. Libraries must also make sure that licensing provisions are in place for properly authenticated remote users, and that adequate help and support for the remote user are provided through more extensive aids on the Web as well as by telephone, e-mail, Internet chat, or other techniques.

ACQUIRING ELECTRONIC RESOURCES

Libraries should play a role in the digital arena similar to that which they play in the print world. The process of acquiring appropriate electronic resources funded through the library should remain the same. Libraries need to be active in selecting the best electronic resources to provide access to authoritative information.

Pricing Models

Vendors use many different types of pricing models. Although e-journals are still largely dominated by fixed subscription-based pricing, pricing variations often arise if a library subscribes to a title in multiple formats (print and electronic). The library's source for a title—directly from a publisher, through an aggregator, or through a serial subscription agent—can also affect price.

One of the greatest challenges facing libraries in dealing with electronic resources and e-journals is understanding how publishers, aggregators, and other information providers charge for electronic access. There are no industry standards about charging for electronic information, and providers use many different pricing mechanisms. Different pricing formulas have pros and cons from the consumer perspective—in this case, the library—and there does not seem to be a universally accepted model. No consensus exists among libraries regarding pricing, other than the universal desire for a model that produces the lowest initial as well as ongoing cost.

Two problems facing libraries are the complexity of pricing models and the need to negotiate pricing with several vendors for a single product. Often, an aggregator and a publisher must each provide pieces of a price. Unclear or disparate definitions in the pricing model in question; effective minimization of costs through group purchases, such as consortia; and alteration of algorithms midstream when conditions change are all critical factors. Following is a summary of some prevalent pricing models, along with their strengths and weaknesses.

FTE Student Counts

The use of full-time-equivalent (FTE) student head counts has become a popular pricing model for academic institutions. For example, CIS has used such pricing techniques for its Universe family of databases with varying degrees of success. A modification on this theme is an FTE count within a particular department in an academic institution for more specialized products that do not have broad campus appeal. This approach has been used by such companies as Engineering Information and for licensing a database, such as IEEE's INSPEC. Most databases that use this pricing model offer volume discounts for larger FTE counts.

Pros   FTE head counts are published by academic institutions and widely accepted as authoritative. Using FTE head counts aggregates part-time students into a uniformly acceptable counting system—typically, 15 credit hours equal one FTE. If volume discounts are offered for larger FTE counts, this model will work well for consortia that want to aggregate users.

Cons   FTE counts do not work for public or corporate libraries. Public libraries, especially in large urban areas, have huge numbers of registered patrons that do not fit well into this paradigm. To solve this problem, some information providers have developed formulas—for example, twenty public library patrons equal one FTE—to make their products more affordable in public library markets. The FTE model requires libraries to purchase products through a "site license" based on an artificial counting system, which forces a library to purchase much more access than is actually required, especially for specialty products.

Pure Head Counts

This pricing model is similar to the FTE method but typically counts raw numbers of users—for example faculty, staff, students, and other registered patrons—to determine a price.

Pros   This model produces more precise counts of actual potential users, as opposed to an artificial aggregation.

Cons   In addition to the same negatives connected to the FTE counting method, doing a pure head count can create artificially high numbers in academic institutions. Many academic institutions are offering growing numbers of courses for part-time students, some taking just one class, who may have little or no use for most of the electronic products being licensed.

Print Plus Fee

When electronic publications, including electronic journals, abstracting and indexing (A&I) services, or directories, have printed counterparts, many publishers tie the price of the electronic version to that of its print equivalent. Some offer access to the online version of the printed publication with no additional fees if the print subscription is retained. Others assess a surcharge for electronic access, typically based on a percentage of the print subscription price. If only electronic access is wanted, pricing algorithms range all the way from a fractional percentage of the print price, on the theory that some of the cost is in printing, handling, and mailing, to the same price as the print or the print price plus a surcharge. Typically, discounts are available for multiyear contracts, larger volume purchases, or consortial deals.

Pros   Using the print price as a base for calculating the price of the electronic version is easily understandable because of the assumption that the majority of the cost in most publications comes from the creation of the intellectual content, editorial work, and formatting. Publishers flexible in negotiating contracts based on this model are often more successful. Some publishers, such as Academic Press, have come up with creative solutions. For example, if a consortium purchases electronic access to the Press's entire suite of electronic journals based on a surcharge to the print subscriptions owned at the time of the deal (the print subscriptions are usually retained in this case), then all members of the consortium gain access to all titles, even those libraries that previously did not maintain subscriptions for the print version.

Cons   The paradigm of coupling electronic access to the print subscription becomes less meaningful if the print version disappears at some point, if there never was a printed edition, or if there are value-added features in the electronic environment. Some publishers have applied very large surcharges to the electronic counterparts.

Concurrent Users

Based on the number of concurrent, or simultaneous, users, this is one of the most popular methods of charging for access to electronic databases, particularly A&I services. It is used less frequently for e-journals. In this type of arrangement, an organization purchases an appropriate number of concurrent users and can add or decrease access as needs change.

Pros   Libraries can scale the purchase of electronic products according to their budget or perceived needs. This allows poorer libraries to have access to a product even if some contention over use takes place during peak times. In this type of pricing scheme, statistics from vendors are very important, because libraries want to scale use based on fact and not on anecdotal information. Concurrent use pricing is widely understood and accepted by most libraries.

Cons   No independent method exists to confirm that the number of purchased concurrent users are actually available at all times. In a Web environment, the meaning of "concurrent user" is not always clear, because by definition it is a stateless condition, and connections are made only briefly to download individual elements. Some vendors do establish underlying "state full" connections with their Web interfaces, so this is less of a conceptual issue. Time-outs need to be carefully set and should be adjustable when possible, because many users do not do formal logoffs. As a result, many idle sessions may be left running.

IP Classes

A few vendors charge by the number of class C or class B Internet Protocol (IP) domains that an institution owns. This method is sometimes coupled with other measures, such as FTE counts.

Pros   This method counts the actual number of nodes available in an organization that could potentially access an electronic resource.

Cons   Having a large IP pool, with many addresses that may not be used, will force organizations to pay for use that may not take place. A large IP pool does not mean that users will go to a licensed resource and may have no relationship to actual use. Distance users accessing electronic databases through commercial Internet Service Providers are not accounted for in this method.

By Transaction, Pay per View, Connect Time, or Retrieval

Charging for database access in a time-sharing environment is often done by connect time, CPU transactions, number of records or articles viewed, or the number of searches launched. Historically, this type of use-based pricing model has been the most popular.

Pros   Use-based pricing is the most accurate method of cost recovery, because charges are based on real and verifiable measures. Pay-per-view access to electronic journal articles has proved to be very popular for some e-journal services, such as Northern Light and inGenta. Many aggregators and publishers are adding a pay-per-article option for individuals or libraries that may have only occasional need for articles and do not require a full annual subscription.

Cons   It is difficult to budget in a use-based environment where costs could quickly escalate beyond an organization's ability to pay. Considerable accounting or system resources may be needed to monitor use for charge-backs.

Other Factors (for example, Total Budget, Materials Budget)

Some products are sold on the basis of the ability of the purchaser to pay, scaled on some measure, such as total organizational budget, materials budget, or number of branches or buildings in a library.

Pros   Some external measurable entity can make it easy to calculate costs and vary those costs as conditions change. H. W. Wilson has historically used this method with different pricing tiers based on a library's budget.

Cons   An organization's ability to pay for a product may have no relationship to a product's value or to the use it may receive. Charging for electronic products based on the number of buildings or branches often unfairly penalizes public or academic libraries with large branch systems, while rewarding more consolidated library systems. Charging for each branch in a library system does not differentiate between a huge central library and many small branches, reading rooms, or storefronts that may have little use for an electronic product.

Dollar Volume Discounts

Some Internet providers reward large-dollar-volume purchases.

Pros   Large-volume discounts favor consortia or very large organizations and encourage libraries to coordinate their purchasing activities.

Cons   Small or consortially unaffiliated libraries are forced to pay top dollar for a product even though they are often least able to pay.

Statewide or Group Discounts

Consortia and statewide purchasing are becoming a major trend in the acquisition of electronic resources.

Pros   Smaller libraries are able to acquire access to many more resources than they would ever be able to afford on their own. Huge volume deals based on overall dollars, concurrent users, FTEs, or other measures often bring the unit cost for access to the lowest possible level. Vendors can make a single sale to a large group and minimize their marketing and training costs.

Cons   Libraries that are unaffiliated with active consortia or are in regions where group deals are not done cannot benefit. It is often politically difficult to coordinate large-scale deals. Some organization must take the fiduciary responsibility for the deal, and there may be risks in obtaining reimbursement from the partners.

The Role of Consortia

Library consortia are hot! Consortia continue to be a driving force in large-scale licensing of electronic resources for libraries. Most libraries have discovered that acquiring electronic resources alone is not cost effective, and that working with a group of other libraries often saves money. The consortial movement itself has been energized by the opportunities possible through collective licensing arrangements for electronic resources, including electronic journals. The International Coalition of Library Consortia (ICOLC), founded in 1997, represents over one hundred major consortia around the world and conducts "meetings dedicated to keeping participating consortia informed about new electronic information resources, pricing practices of electronic providers and vendors, and other issues of importance to directors and governing boards of consortia."[1] Another indicator of the growth and importance of the consortial movement was the establishment, in 1999, of a new journal called *Library Consortium Management: An International Journal.*

Collective Licensing Benefits

Consortial licensing agreements are meant to benefit libraries and provide features that may not be fully attainable by an individual organization. The power of collective bargaining has not only brought benefits on specific contracts, but also changed the marketplace. In March 1998, the International Coalition of Library Consortia published a Statement of Current and Preferred Practices for Selection and Purchase of Electronic Information that set a standard for guidelines in consortial licensing.[2] Another excellent Web resource on licensing is available at Yale University's Liblicense.[3]

Key features that libraries and consortia prefer in their licensing arrangements include:

1. Substantial discounts for bringing a block of business at one time
2. No-cost or low-cost access to electronic products for small libraries or others in a group that would normally not purchase a product, but could marginally benefit from a group purchase
3. Reasonable provisions for interlibrary loan, printing, and downloading that reflect the real world
4. Licensing that is flexible enough to handle multitype consortia, including academic, public, school, and special libraries
5. Contracts that limit risk on price increases
6. Contracts that protect the privacy of users
7. Contracts that offer useful statistics
8. Pricing variations for consortia, single institutions, and individuals
9. Clear and rapid recourse for system problems and response-time issues
10. Compliance with standards where appropriate
11. Hours of service guarantee
12. Cataloging copy for full-text embedded within aggregations

The Power of Cooperation

The leveraging of financial resources from many libraries through a consortium should result in a win-win situation for the library, the publisher, and the aggregator. The power of cooperation will result in lowered costs for particular electronic resources and maximize the buying power for each library. One contract guaranteeing access for an entire region will benefit both libraries and publishers, and offer a consistent set of rules within a region so that each library is not working under different contract options.

Contract Issues and Challenges

Consortial agreements for electronic resources do not always come easily. The problems tend to be political and economic rather than technical, and some of the greatest challenges include the following:

Obtaining agreement on what contracts to pursue. So many opportunities are available in the marketplace that consortia must focus efforts on contracts that will benefit their members the most while not completely ignoring niche products or less-expensive deals.

Pooling financial resources unless the consortium has its own funding. Vendors often require a single point of billing, so that a consortium may need to "front" money for its members until the central billing agency is reimbursed.

Purchasing some products as a single collective asset, and, if individual libraries each contribute, allocating costs back to the members.

Stopping the "crabbiest" member in a group from killing or slowing down deals.

Clustering purchases. In a large, heterogeneous consortium, very few products are of universal interest. One technique to solve this problem is to cluster purchases within a larger group. Only those libraries that are interested in a particular product need play and pay. Most publishers and vendors recognize the need for purchasing clusters within a consortium.

Keeping contracts simple. Complex contracts are sometimes required, but common sense should prevail. Artificial requirements that cannot be upheld in actual practice should be excluded from contracts. For example, walk-in patrons to a library should always be allowed to use a product, even if they are not among the library's primary clientele. Interlibrary loan provisions should be fair, and printing provisions should be allowed. Both the seller and the buyer should be reasonable and practical in their expectations.

ACCESSING ELECTRONIC RESOURCES

Organizing electronic resources in a way meaningful for local users will help point them to vetted, quality information.

User Interface Issues and Trends

Because no publisher or aggregator offers a complete suite of services, libraries and their users will be faced with different interfaces and search engines. One major trend is to allow the linking of full-text journal articles from within abstracting and indexing (A&I) services. The chief difficulty with this arrangement is that it often works only when the user stays within the same family of products—OCLC or Ovid, for example. Some vendors are working on broader solutions within their A&I offerings, such as SilverPlatter's SilverLinker or Ovid's OpenLinks, but even if these are acquired and configured, they still may not meet every need. Different user interfaces also create challenges for reference and bibliographic instruction.

The overlap of e-journals within collections (for example, EBSCO, IAC/Gale, Northern Light, Electric Library, Dialog@CARL, CIS, Bell & Howell ProQuest) has also become a major problem for libraries. Libraries frequently purchase the same content from several vendors because of overlap within collections, and, as a result, confusion reigns among users.

Another major challenge facing libraries is to determine when e-journals should be cataloged and hotlinked from within the local OPAC, and when they should be put in an institutional Web site listing. Most libraries try to catalog electronic serials for which a formal subscription exists; however, handling full-text e-journal titles embedded within aggregations, such as EBSCO, ProQuest, or IAC/Galenet, has become problematic. Some aggregators are beginning to supply MARC cataloging records for their collections so that libraries may load these into their local OPACS. E-journals that are "on trial" are usually not cataloged because of the effort involved, although most organizations list titles in this category on their institutional Web pages.

Noncommercial E-journal Web Sites

Several organizations have developed wonderful listings of electronic serials that are available on the Web. Commercial aggregators and serial
jobbers often have excellent listings and frequently include article-by-
article abstracting and indexing for the journal titles in their portfolio
(usually supplied by publishers). A major drawback to these commercial
listings, however, is that they are sometimes available only to the particular aggregator's customers. Such lists typically contain only e-journals
sold by that aggregator and, thus, exclude many free sources on the Web
as well as titles for which the jobber does not have distribution rights.
To fill this gap, many libraries and organizations have developed their
own listing of e-journals on the Web. These Web sites can be valuable
tools for the end user as well as librarians involved with reference, cataloging, and acquisitions.[4] A selected list of sites of particular interest
may be found in the appendix at the end of this chapter.

Authentication and Authorization

User authentication and authorization have long been issues for the computing community. However, as libraries and other organizations have
begun to develop a more comprehensive, networked vision of information
access over the Internet, including widescale access to electronic journals,
it has become clear that flexible new solutions need to be implemented.
Players in this drama must include the library patron, the library itself, the
information provider, and, sometimes, other parties. Further complicating
the environment is the involvement of many libraries in consortia, which
are actively taking part not only in providing services but also in broker-
ing deals for member libraries in order to save money.

The goal of user authentication and authorization is to let valid parties access databases and information services from anywhere at any
time, without making the process too difficult for the library, the information provider, or the patron. Clifford Lynch, executive director of the
Coalition for Networked Information, has written an excellent
overview of the history of authentication as well as current challenges.[5]

Most libraries currently offer electronic information from a wide
variety of sources. Some, such as libraries' online catalogs, are openly
accessible to all. Others, such as networked CD-ROMs, electronic journals from a variety of publishers or aggregators, various indexing and
abstracting services from remote providers (OCLC FirstSearch, Gale,
Bell & Howell, Dialog@CARL), and locally mounted databases (Silver-
Platter, Ovid, OCLC SiteSearch) require user authentication and authorization. To further complicate matters, libraries want to provide access

to electronic sources not only from workstations in the library and in campus buildings, but also from users' offices, dormitories, and homes. Some organizations provide their own dial-in modem pools, which would likely have the same network identity as on-campus workstations, but many organizations do not. In fact, some organizations are beginning to outsource dial-in service to commercial organizations, and many valid patrons have selected commercial Internet Service Providers, such as AOL, CompuServe, MSN, or EarthLink, further complicating the authentication and authorization process.

Most libraries use their World Wide Web home pages to list which electronic resources are available and to explain how these resources can be accessed. It is also common to explain on the library Web pages the access restrictions that apply as well as the complexities caused by authorization and authentication challenges.

A number of general solutions for authentication are commonly in use, each with its own benefits and limitations. Many libraries now offer electronic resource authentication through a local integrated library system (ILS) developed by an ILS vendor. These solutions are particularly attractive because they usually use the existing circulation patron file as the source of users so no additional systems need to be developed. Examples include Web Access Management from Innovative Interfaces Inc., using a Proxy server, and Web Checker from CARL Corporation, using a referring URL. Examples of some of the common approaches follow.

IP Filtering

This technique uses an Internet Protocol (IP) address, or a range of addresses, to filter access to a database or service so that only authorized users may gain access. This IP filtering may be done on the same server where the information resides, or it may be done on some other server before the user gets to the end point. This solution is very easy to implement. For example, a whole institutional class B or set of class C IP domains can be authenticated at once. From the user perspective, there are no passwords to remember, there is no need to give out passwords to others, and the library does not need to manage a large set of dynamically changing passwords. If, however, the user is using a commercial ISP that does not have the same network domain as the institution, IP filtering fails. This means that the patron must either come to the campus or into the library to gain access, or must dial-in through an institutional modem pool and not use the commercial ISP. Although IP filtering is one of the most widely used techniques, if used alone, it fails the test of "access from anywhere." A library has partially failed if a user must be physically present at the institution and cannot use the resources from a remote location through a commercial ISP.

ID Login and Password

The computing community has used logins and passwords as the primary access technique for many years. Upon reaching an IP site, the user is asked to log in for access. To improve security, passwords must be changed periodically to curtail the number of unauthorized users. Although this technique works well, it has many challenges: (1) the issuing of logins/passwords can be a huge job, especially in a larger library setting (frequently users are asked to use their library ID card number); (2) passwords can be distributed by patrons to unauthorized users; (3) if random logins/passwords are issued, they are often forgotten; and (4) unless logins/passwords are handled through a gateway or proxy server, a user may end up with many passwords for different systems.

Proxy Servers

In this technique, a user must log in or pass an IP filter into an intermediate server that is automatically known by the end IP as passing a legitimate user. Basically, users on one machine are allowed to be passed to another. This technique has been widely used, especially for telnet or Z39.50 connections where users take on the identity of the last server they passed through. Although this technique is possible in the Web environment, it is much more difficult. In a traditional Web connection, a user typically retains the network identity of his or her browser. To use a proxy server on the Web, each Web browser must have the proxy server identified in its "preferences" section. Proxies have several limitations: (1) they can become a single point of failure in an organization, so that if the proxy is down, access to all users is completely cut off; (2) proxy servers require that all requests be handled twice, resulting in extra overhead in computer processing and sometimes extra response time problems; (3) in a Web environment, one must specially configure a browser to use a proxy rather than going directly to the end provider; and (4) proxy solutions work when the user has a clearly defined "parent organization." This can be problematic for patrons who have multiple affiliations, or for libraries that are members of different consortia or societies.

Electronic Certificates

The Internet Engineering Task Force (IETF) and others are working on various types of electronic certificates for authentication purposes. Standard X509 uses a technique in which the person (workstation) in possession of this digital object has this name (where name is interpreted rather loosely, and might include a public cryptographic key that the individual can use to sign documents) . . . [T]he traditional use of certificates is for authentication and not authorization. There are provisions to carry user attributes in X509 Version 3 certificates, for example, but there are no standards on what attributes should be carried or how to interpret them.[6]

Typically, an electronic certificate would carry enough information so that a user could be authorized against a central database for access to a suite of resources. Both Netscape and Microsoft are beginning to incorporate electronic certificate software in their browsers as this type of need grows.

Referring URL

The referring URL approach requires that a user be authenticated on a local server and then "passed on" to a remote system that has been configured to accept the referral. Because there are no proxy server URLs to be set in a browser, no digital certificates to manage or lose, and no special logins/passwords to manage, this arrangement is very easy to use. The primary challenge is that each information provider must support referring URLs, and these arrangements must be made on a vendor-by-vendor basis.

Statistics

According to the International Coalition of Library Consortia,

> the use of licensed electronic information resources will continue to expand and in some cases become the sole or dominant means of access to content. The electronic environment, as manifested by the World Wide Web, provides an opportunity to improve the measurement of the use of these resources. In the electronic arena we can more accurately determine which information is being accessed and used. Without violating any issues of privacy or confidentiality we can dramatically enhance our understanding of information use.[7]

The collection and dissemination of use statistics for electronic resources, particularly electronic serials, is key for most libraries. Statistical data can be valuable for guiding purchase decisions, supporting networking infrastructure, allocating costs in a consortium or to departments, assisting in determining where more emphasis should be placed for reference and instruction, and even prioritizing cataloging backlogs.

Ideally, libraries would prefer a Web-based ad hoc statistical interface that would allow them to get the exact information in a user-defined format when it is needed. Although different kinds of use data may be relevant for different products and interfaces, such data might include the following elements:

Number of queries by database (or serial title)

Number of queries by IP address/locator, account or password, institution

Number of sessions (logins)

Number of items examined (marked, downloaded, e-mailed, printed)

Use level by time period (with user-defined granularity)

Peak concurrent use (if appropriate)

Total hours of server downtime in a given period

Archiving

The issues surrounding archiving and perpetual access to electronic resources are broad and complex. Analyses of the challenges surrounding electronic resource archiving are available in the published literature and at the Web sites of key organizations, such as the Coalition for Networked Information, the American Library Association, and the Council on Library and Information Resources.[8] Archiving and perpetual access, which is not necessarily the same as archiving, involve such questions as:

What if a publisher or aggregator disappears? Will continued access to electronic information be available?

What if a subscription ceases? Will an organization have continued access to an electronic backfile for which it has already paid? How much will this cost?

What about changing media, storage formats, and markup formats? How will continued access be ensured?

How should organizations handle data security? How will data backups, off-site storage, and mirroring Web sites be handled?

Reliability

The network is crucial for access to all electronic information. Without a healthy Internet, access to all electronic data will be difficult or impossible. Response-time problems can be caused by any element in a complex chain, including the broader Internet, the server operated by the information provider, the reliability of the institutional network, and the local workstation. Although it is often difficult to identify why access to some electronic resources is substandard, a number of practical solutions may help improve poor reliability and accessibility. Libraries may want to examine such opportunities as:

> Asking an information provider to "mirror" the Web site. Major providers often do this to offer redundancy, split traffic, and provide closer proximity to users (from a network perspective).

> Considering dedicated leased lines for access if a particular service is mission critical and Internet access is a problem. Many larger libraries do this with OCLC for cataloging purposes.

> Considering the use of multiple Internet Service Providers (ISPs) either on the vendor or library side. Although many libraries do not have a choice in this area because Internet access is provided by a parent institution, the addition of a second ISP may bring a library and an electronic resource closer together on the network, thus offering fewer "hops" on the Internet and better service.

> Mounting locally some electronic journals, indexing/abstracting services, and other electronic resources. If a library can afford this in terms of human resources, finances, and technical expertise, the local mounting of electronic products may make sense.

CONCLUSION

Libraries have an exciting future as the digital age emerges. Although some roles will change, many will remain the same. Librarians must think globally but act locally. They must be creative, pay attention to details, have a cooperative attitude, and maintain a positive outlook. They should keep informed, get involved at the local and national levels, and, whenever possible, comply with standards. Librarians need to be flexible, adjust work flows and staffing to accommodate change, and work with others for best pricing. The printed world will be with us for many years, but embracing changes and incorporating them into our new, electronic world will keep libraries viable.

NOTES

1. From "About the International Coalition of Library Consortia." See: http://www.library.yale.edu/consortia/

2. See: http://www.library.yale.edu/consortia/statement.html

3. See: http://www.library.yale.edu/~llicense/index.shtml

4. For a more complete listing of major commercial and noncommercial e-journal Web sites, go to Electronic Journal Access at http://www.coalliance.org/ejournal

5. Clifford A. Lynch, "Authentication and Authorization, Part I. The Changing Role in a Networked Information Environment," *Library Hi Tech* 15, no. 1–2 (no. 57–58) (1997): 30–38.

6. Ibid., 35.

7. International Coalition of Library Consortia, *Guidelines for Statistical Measures of Usage of Web-based Indexed, Abstracted and Full Text Resources* (November 1998). See: http://www.library.yale.edu/consortia/webstats.html

8. See: http://www.cni.org; http://www.ala.org; and http://www.clir.org

APPENDIX
Selected Lists of Electronic Serials

Electronic Journal Access
Colorado Alliance of Research Libraries
http://www.coalliance.org/ejournal

Managed by the nonprofit Colorado Alliance of Research Libraries, this site provides one of the best general-purpose listings of electronic journals on the Web. It contains almost 10,000 titles available directly from publishers, professional societies, or smaller entities. It generally excludes titles embedded within aggregations.

NewJour: Electronic Journals and Serials
http://gort.ucsd.edu/newjour/

This is the Web archive of the NewJour electronic discussion list and provides a listing of new serial publications on the Internet. This Web site is mounted at the University of California, San Diego (UCSD), but is actually the collaborative effort of many librarians at different institutions.

CIC Electronic Journals Collection
http://ejournals.cic.net/

The Committee on Institutional Cooperation (CIC) Electronic Journals Collection is a prototype electronic journal management system coordinated by the librarians of the CIC member universities and the staff of CICNet, Inc. At present, the site lists freely available e-journals that have been archived by the CIC. The CIC is the academic consortium of the members of the Big Ten athletic conference (Midwest United States) and the University of Chicago.

Enews.com
http://www.enews.com

Although this is a commercial Web site, it contains listings of popular magazines that are freely available over the Web.

Australian Journals Online
http://www.nla.gov.au/oz/ausejour.html

Australian Journals Online is a listing of over 1,700 Australian electronic journals, magazines, Webzines, newsletters, and e-mail fanzines. It includes both local and overseas works with Australian content, authorship, or emphasis as well as entries for sites that advertise or promote Australian journals.

Electronic Journals and Serials
University of Buffalo Libraries
http://ublib.buffalo.edu/libraries/e-resources/ejournals/

This selective list of electronic journals, maintained by the librarians at the University of Buffalo Libraries, is an excellent example of a special project done in an academic setting.

Jake
Yale University School of Medicine
http://jake.med.yale.edu

Jake supports the management of and linking between online resources, and lists electronic journals that are embedded within aggregations from over 150 suppliers. Jake consists of a database containing information about e-resources, including online journals, databases, search interfaces, and textbooks, and how they relate to each other. These relationships include a functional but minimal amount of title authority control, listing of indexing and full-text coverage, and resource evolution. Jake is free for anyone to use, modify, copy, or redistribute under the terms of the GNU General Public License (GPL).

6

Seven Common Myths about Acquiring and Accessing E-journals

DAN TONKERY

The rapid growth of the Internet and the various technologies supporting this tool have raised everyone's interest in finding ways to harness this new, almost unlimited, power. Not only have the academic and professional communities signed on to the Internet phenomenon, but the entire consumer community has bought into the promise as well. Most notable is the growth and high valuation of the dot.com companies. Everyone sees a pot of gold at the end of this rainbow, and many librarians view this new medium as the answer to their fiscal woes.

In the library community, where most of us work or sell products, the end users' acceptance of the Internet is universal. Libraries of all sizes and disciplines are adopting Internet services and are being pressured to make more of these services available. Faculty and students are looking to the library to lead the Internet revolution on campus. More access is now the cry, and the pressure is quickly mounting for direct access by end users, with the library playing a central role as the filter by supporting public access to the Internet through the OPAC and by arranging for and paying for the wide range of information services.

Based on a presentation at the First Electronic Serials Institute, "A Capital Idea: Electronic Serials from Acquisition to Access," September 26–27, 1997, Washington, D.C. The opinions expressed are strictly those of the author and do not represent any corporate viewpoint.

The faculty, the university administration, and the students all want desktop access and have great difficulty understanding why that is not immediately possible. Now that everything is online and available over the Internet, why continue to invest in print publications? On some campuses, the question being asked is: Why continue to invest in the traditional library at all? Few understand the level of difficulty that librarians face when trying to acquire the access rights to many of the popular publisher services, such as Academic Press's Ideal or Link from Springer-Verlag. Not only is there often a long negotiation process, but in the end, access to an electronic format is by no means free; often the cost is an added drain on an already limited library budget. Faculty as well as students have trouble understanding why everything on the Net is not free.

Faculty are not the only ones confused about e-journals and the access process. In the past two years, literally hundreds of meetings have been devoted to e-journals in the library market; the amount of misinformation coming out of those meetings is embarrassing. This chapter looks at some of the common myths surrounding the acquisition of and access to e-journals and tries to set the record straight.

MYTH NO. 1

Publishers Are Rushing to Convert Their Print Journals to E-journal Form to Reduce Costs

Of all the messages, this one is clearly offtrack and downright wrong. Publishers of all sizes are rushing to convert their print journals into e-journals, but cost reduction is not driving the conversion race. Many publishers do not have information technology departments with the sophistication required to support the Internet from a software, hardware, or telecommunications standpoint. For a publisher to begin the conversion process, the company must either build up the skill set internally or contract the work out to a systems house. So far, most publishers have taken the contract route and are buying the technical skills to develop search engines and Web site hosting, and the technical support needed to convert the paper format to an electronic format. Put it all together, and no publisher will suggest that the exercise of moving to the Internet is less costly than producing a paper product.

On the contrary, the process of converting print products to electronic form and providing desktop access via the Internet is a very expensive one. From the publisher's standpoint, investment resources are required to build this new product or service, while the expenses associated with maintaining the paper products continue. All the costs of production are still active while the conversion to the electronic format takes place. Even after the conversion process is finished, the publisher still has expenses related to marketing, editorial, and peer review as well as major overhead expenses. Maintaining a foot in both the print and the electronic worlds is expensive, and someone must pay this cost.

Shifting to an all-electronic world is not possible at this time. Many of the paper-based journals are cash cows and produce a profit. There is no established revenue stream for the electronic products, and going with an all-electronic product is an unwise business risk for a publisher to take at this early stage of e-journal development.

At the same time, the more success an e-journal product enjoys, the more pressure there is to produce more e-journal products, with the result that the e-journal may indeed cause the demise of the paper product and possibly of the publisher as well. Publishers are not technology leaders, and few are willing to take major business risks in these uncharted waters. In fact, a number of publishers have reviewed the current scene and have decided that it is now time to get out of the business, because no clear revenue stream can be foreseen without a serious investment of new capital. Many do not have the resources to undertake this effort and are following the philosophy of "take the money and run."

On the other hand, some publishers are moving into the e-journal world to keep up with the competition, because the fear of being left behind or left out is very strong. At no time have publishers approached an e-journal project as a strategy for reducing costs. They recognize that this is a very expensive undertaking, that they must be willing to commit significant resources to move into the electronic market, and that the success of the e-journal may hasten the decline of the print journal. At the same time, the process of obtaining access to the e-journals from the publishers is convoluted and expensive. In the end, everyone is in favor of desktop delivery, but the costs associated with such service are still very high and a labor of love on everyone's part.

MYTH NO. 2

E-journals Will Solve the Serials Pricing Crisis in Libraries

There is a broad-based misconception that it is cheaper to deliver a desktop article than a paper product. Today that is not quite true. If a publisher were beginning without any print history or obligation to subscribers of a print product, then perhaps it would be advantageous to deliver information only in an electronic format. However, some libraries still want the traditional print product, while a growing number of libraries are satisfied with just the electronic format, and thus publishers and libraries are trapped in both the old and the new worlds at the same time. Until we can get to the point where the electronic format is the preferred delivery mechanism, we are looking at an expensive dual system of publishing paid for by the end users, which in many cases is the library. As a result, the price of a subscription includes the cost of the traditional publishing model, plus the investment cost of moving into the desktop delivery field as well as a share of any losses resulting from cancellations of print subscriptions.

The popularity of e-journals should not be expected to remedy the rapid increase in serials pricing that has eroded the budgets of many institutions. The serials pricing crisis has been a concern for many years, and it will not be resolved simply by a short-term shift to electronic formats. Rather, we will continue to see price increases for paper products along with the expanded availability of e-journals, forcing libraries to move into the electronic world. At best, the price of e-journals has been tied to the cost of paper subscriptions. A number of publishers have supported a pricing model in which an e-journal can be obtained for an added percentage of the cost of the paper subscription, and, though that seems simple from the client's perspective, the library still must come up with the extra 30 to 40 percent required to purchase the e-journal.

Opportunities for savings may be available if a library can obtain access to electronic journals through a consortial purchase. Consortia sales enable a publisher to simplify the acquisitions process and, at the same time, to increase market share. At one time, consortium purchases were particularly advantageous for smaller members of the group, and, though the cost differential may be less beneficial today than it was in the past, smaller institutions may still find that a consortial purchase is cost effective. Larger members of a consortium may find that they can sometimes negotiate a more favorable arrangement directly with a publisher, rather than obtaining access through a consortium. For the time being, and regardless of the way in which libraries acquire site licenses and provide access to the growing number of e-journals, they still need to maintain subscriptions to paper journals.

Acquiring the e-journal is not simply a matter of having sufficient funds for acquisition. The growing number of e-journals will not lower operating costs or save the institution any real money. If anything, the cost of acquiring e-journals will go up, both in terms of actual dollars spent for site licenses as well as for overhead for support from staff who deal with the acquisition and licensing of the material and who conduct training sessions and provide end-user support. The extra resources needed to properly support the e-journal infrastructure in public access, cataloging, and systems can add a considerable financial burden to an already overburdened organization.

When all is said and done, the cost of e-journals will continue to rise as the demand for desktop delivery of information climbs. Libraries are facing a major growth period in online usage for e-journals—and e-books are just a half-step away and coming on strong. Rather than contributing to a speedy resolution to the serials pricing crisis in libraries, the growth of e-journals, and e-products in general, is going to make major demands on library budgets.

MYTH NO. 3
Acquiring and Processing E-journals Requires Fewer Staff Than Does Acquiring Traditional Materials

Anyone working in a library today knows what this myth is all about. The acquisitions process for any e-journal is long, expensive, and overly complex. The cost comparison between ordering a print journal and subscribing to an e-journal for campuswide access is a factor of ten to one if not fifty to one. In the traditional print world, there is an ordering process with databases of available titles arranged by subject or topic, and with clear pricing according to location or geographic area. For the acquisition of the e-journal, however, nothing is simple and straightforward. The title could be part of a publisher's offering that includes the entire stable of titles, and, to obtain one or two desired titles, the library must buy the entire file. Then comes the pricing battle. For the library to obtain a "real" price, the publisher requires an entire set of data based on the institution's projected use of the e-journal. In most cases, the library is not acquiring the title in the same way it would acquire a print publication; rather, the library is leasing access to the title. The lease, however, comes with a string of limitations and restrictions. In order for the library to arrange access to the publication, a lease or licensing agreement has to be executed and reviewed by the institution's legal staff. After the library's lawyers finish their review, the agreement will be returned for review by the publisher's legal team. The paperwork could change hands a number of times, as the two groups of attorneys make changes and counterchanges to the licensing agreement. After weeks or perhaps even months, both parties will finally sign an agreement, and access to the title might become a reality.

With a valid licensing agreement in hand, the next hurdle to be overcome is that of having the publisher's technical staff code the library's access rights into the system and actually turn on the access rights. If access is achieved by the third attempt, a library should consider itself lucky. Just getting someone to respond to voice-mail messages is a sign of privilege. From the time the decision to acquire the title is made until all the necessary documents have been signed and access has been established, three to six months may elapse.

Neither publishers nor subscription agents are organized to support the ordering of e-journals in a cost-efficient manner. Instead, the work seems to have been delegated to the library at a time when the library can least support it. Most libraries have limited staff, and many have experienced reductions in technical services, where much of the negotiation and contact with suppliers takes place. Arranging for access and managing e-journals are time-consuming and ever-changing processes that should and could easily be automated to take full advantage of today's technology. Instead, the acquisition of e-journals continues to be tied to a primitive process set up by each publisher, with scant regard either for efficient service or for a library's staffing problems.

MYTH NO. 4

E-journals Will Be Delivered to the Individual Desktop, Reducing the Need for Public Services Staff

With today's technology, there is no question that it is possible to deliver over 2,500 journals to the desktop without a great deal of staff intervention. However, the library still plays a central role in identifying available e-journals, providing accurate links to the publications, and providing access to the e-journal collection. Public services staff members are often involved in selecting e-journals for the collection, in training users on the intricacies of different front ends, and in keeping the library Web site up-to-date.

Even though it may sometimes seem as if everything is now online or on the Web, the reality is that in most libraries, a great deal of information is not yet online, and librarians must still rely on a large volume of valuable material in paper format to answer reference questions and do research. It is the role of the public services staff to educate users on how to get the most information out of these two parallel universes. Public services staff must keep the end users up-to-date about the variety of services the library offers, and make sure that users are successful in finding answers to their questions, whether through the real or the electronic realm. In addition, many public services staff members have taken on additional duties as Webmasters, with responsibility for keeping e-journal information and links up-to-date.

Before libraries rush to reassign public services staff to positions in other areas of the library, it is important to remember that the paper and the electronic environments will continue to coexist for a number of years to come. The variety of search engines and the many different interfaces available for users are causing public services staff to struggle to keep up with developments. For the moment, real savings in staff time with the conversion from print to electronic will not be realized. Eventually, more unmediated information will be available to users from the desktop, but the need for skilled public services staff in the library will continue for the foreseeable future.

MYTH NO. 5

The Costs of E-journals Will Be Passed to the End Users, Thus Saving Acquisitions Funds

Building digital libraries and digital collections is a new challenge for many institutions. In some states, the legislature is providing separate funding for state institutions to purchase digital collections, thus giving libraries in those institutions access to a statewide contract without having to resort to using limited library resources. State plans such as these recognize that the gap between the more-affluent libraries and the less-affluent libraries is widening, and the hope is that by providing access to important digital collections, the quality of education in a region of a state, or even throughout a state, will improve.

The University of California has set up a virtual campus with responsibility for systemwide contract negotiations and for assisting libraries with the purchase of digital collections and major publisher products, such as Science Direct or Academic Press's Ideal. Funding for these types of initiatives comes from state and university sources, and supports the acquisition of e-journals and databases without impacting the libraries' budget allocation.

Supporting the acquisition of e-journals by obtaining funding from sources outside the library, such as a state legislature, is one thing, but charging the end user for access is problematic. In many academic institutions, obtaining access to research overhead funds is increasingly difficult. Researchers hold on to that source of funds, yet still expect support for campuswide information requirements to come from the library's general acquisitions budget. Although there might be new money for technology on many campuses, buying e-journals is a hard sell at best. Universities see as their responsibility the need to supply telecommunications capacity to the campus and to update the computer network, but most are unwilling to fund specific e-journals projects, as they benefit only small pockets of researchers.

In an academic setting, another potential source of revenue may come from the students themselves, not on a transaction basis, but in the form of student fees. Several institutions around the country have implemented a student activity fee designated specifically for library services. Each term, every student pays a small amount earmarked for the library, with the promise that the funds will be used to keep the library up-to-date with the latest technology. This is just one method libraries might investigate to obtain additional funding. No matter what, libraries should not plan to charge the end users directly for access to e-journals. Each institution must determine the priority for access and make the budget support the activity. Do not expect the end users to cover the cost of e-journal services.

MYTH NO. 6

Libraries Prefer to Order E-journals Directly from the Publisher

This is one of those strange myths that must have been started by publishers in order to maintain control over the e-journal access process. Nothing could be farther from the truth. In fact, there is no compelling argument for publishers to handle the ordering process themselves. For over fifty years, libraries have been ordering subscriptions from agents, and they see little reason to return to the model of ordering directly from publishers. Libraries would much rather order e-journals from the subscription vendor with whom they have a long-term, established relationship.

Subscription agents have successfully ordered materials for libraries in a variety of formats, from print to CD-ROM, for several generations, and they should have no trouble processing orders for e-journals. Such agents as Faxon have built e-journal databases with links to the publishers, the license agreement, and the latest pricing information. An agent should go through a certification process with a publisher, and any order coming from that agent would be recognized and entered as valid. The agent takes the responsibility to verify that the license is signed and that the terms are agreed upon.

Libraries would like to have quick response to their orders, ideally with the service turned on the same day as the request was received! A library staff member should be able to e-mail the agent and provide the details for the order, and the agent should be able to order the item and activate service all in the same day. Instead, libraries continue to struggle with the ordering and activation process, becoming more and more frustrated with the poor quality of service being provided by publishers.

MYTH NO. 7
The Digital Library Requires Skills beyond Traditional Training

There is no question that libraries are going though a period of rapid change, and that the Internet and the Web are changing the nature and character of many library positions. In the past, when new library staff members were hired, the focus was on having expertise in two or more foreign languages or on having a subject masters or an M.B.A. Now, we expect Web expertise with PURL or Oracle and familiarity with computer programming languages. No doubt, in the future, librarians will need an even wider range of skills. The best source of this talent lies within our own organizations, and we need to provide training for our existing staff members and reward those individuals with technical skills or aptitude. The job market for those with technical skills is hot, and libraries should take care not to lose highly skilled staff trained in computer-related areas. There is little need to hire staff from nonlibrary professions. Rather, we should find and train the brightest in our profession. Libraries have within their walls staff eager to learn and move ahead. Librarians should not be counted out of the new age.

CONCLUSION

The acquisition of e-journals is expensive and time-consuming. Adhering to the model of acquiring e-journals directly from the publishers is counterproductive to users as well as to library staff. We need to work together as an industry to reduce the order processing time, so that a library can identify an e-journal title and have every reason to expect the service to be activated within forty-eight hours or less. We have the most modern technology to support our information needs, but are willing to compromise on a primitive method to establish an order for an electronic journal. How could we come so far and still hold on to our near-prehistoric ordering methods? E-journals will be part of our future, and libraries should anticipate ever-increasing costs.

7

How Intellectual Property Laws Affecting Libraries Are Changing

SARAH E. SULLY

How do we guarantee free thought when the push is to propertize every idea?[1]

[R]efusing to make a profit is a rejection of God's will.[2]

With the advent of e-resources of all types, serials librarians are realizing that they must add licensing practice to their portfolio of skills. Even those librarians fortunate enough to have legal advisors working with them need to know the ins and outs of license agreements. Some are embracing this fact, some are not.[3] Regardless of one's preferences, licensing is here for the foreseeable future.

As we accept the era of licensed versus owned resources, the lexicon of copyright law is increasingly a part of the library world. Once able to rely on a grounding in such topics as the first-sale doctrine and *Williams & Wilkins,* librarians must now be fluent in such issues as whether a display of a work is "in the course of face-to-face teaching activities," and whether e-ILL constitutes infringement of one of the six exclusive rights of the copyright owner.[4] To assist in the growing awareness of copyright arcana, it may be helpful to ask these questions: Where is copyright law going? What recent developments should librarians be aware of? What things should they be watching out for? This chapter attempts to shed a little light on these questions.

The author is grateful to Richard Andrews and Colette Brown for their assistance in the preparation of this chapter.

TRENDS

Copyright law is in the process, and has been since its beginnings, of re-alizing its potential under capitalism, through an ever-increasing expan-sion of the rights of copyright owners. The trend is manifest in an increasing commodification of works of authorship, at ever-increasing levels of granularity, coupled with the capitalistic drive to monetize each discernible part, for longer periods of time.[5] Under our economic sys-tem, copyrightable works are on an inexorable path away from any em-phasis on personal authorship, and becoming "nothing more than [carriers] of market value."[6] Rather than polemicize this discussion (though it's arguable that something is fundamentally out of balance in the notion of for-profit corporations, with their bottom line goal of in-creasing shareholder value, marketing to the not-for-profit library com-munity), the following sections will look at how this trend may be discerned in recent legislative and other developments. One may be bet-ter equipped to deal with this pernicious trend if one is armed with knowledge about it.[7]

UCITA

> *[T]he UCC2B Committee is positioning itself*
> *to be the instrument of that greed.*[8]

The Uniform Computer Information Transactions Act, or UCITA, is be-coming the law. The act has been signed into law in the Commonwealth of Virginia to take effect in July 2001, has passed the legislature of the state of Maryland, and has been introduced in four other states and the District of Columbia.[9] UCITA is now well enough known that we may forgo a history of how it got here.[10] Likewise, a discussion of all that it portends for librarians is beyond the scope of this chapter.[11] How UCITA fits into the theory of the ever-increasing drive to recognize mon-etary value from works of authorship is the focus here.

The purpose of UCITA is to clarify rights with respect to e-contracting. Though not a copyright statute per se, the act raises many questions with respect to how it will interplay with U.S. copyright law.[12] Can copyright law be preempted by contracts between private parties? If so, fair use, the first-sale doctrine, and the other limitations on the exclusive rights of copyright owners set forth in sections 107 through 112 of the U.S. Copyright Act could be eliminated or restricted by contracts. Or, do these limitations, set forth in federal copyright law, trump state law (such as UCITA) as well as private contracts? The answer is unclear and is not made clearer in UCITA.[13] Furthermore, recent case law suggests that there is reason for concern.[14]

UCITA is a difficult, dense statute to parse. Analyses of UCITA from the standpoint of licensing practice almost always begin with the scope of the statute. It is incredibly broad. The drafters of the act intend to sweep not only licensed software within its purview, but all rights in "computer information."[15] This definition will include nearly all electronic content with few exceptions. Although the exact contours of the act's applicability may not yet be perfectly clear, it certainly encompasses e-serials as well as databases. Unless the parties to a contract opt out of the act's application, license agreements for these resources in general will be governed by this law.[16]

The licensor bias of UCITA has been discussed aplenty.[17] There are myriad ways, large and small, throughout the statute, that the default position is the one favoring the licensor of informational content. Following are just a few of the more salient clauses of the statute that licensors will use to their advantage, and of which licensees should be aware.

Hidden License Terms

UCITA validates the "clickwrap" license, the kind that appears on a computer screen and invites the reader to click a box with the words "I Agree," thereby making that person a licensee.[18] These agreements may be separated from the registration screen, home page, or other screen of a Web site that a user is viewing, requiring that the user hit a link (such as "Please read the License") in order to view the agreement.[19] How prominent must the link be? The practice sometimes seen on Web sites of placing a small link to the license at the bottom of the home page is probably sufficient, because the standard is that the link be "conspicuous," which is defined as "so written, displayed, or presented that a reasonable person . . . ought to have noticed it."[20] There is no requirement that a licensee actually review a license agreement, but only that she or he have an opportunity to review it; that opportunity can even come after payment for the information has occurred.[21]

Gap Filler Terms

UCITA's terms are set up as "gap fillers," a holdover from the act's origins in the Uniform Commercial Code. This means that if the parties to a license agreement have negotiated certain terms and memorialized those terms in their agreement, any corresponding terms of UCITA do not come into play. Rather, much of UCITA applies only when terms are left out of a license agreement. In that case, UCITA's terms will fill the gap in the agreement and dictate what happens in the event a question or dispute arises with respect to the missing term. An example of a gap filler term that librarians will want to watch out for is section 109, Choice of Law. What happens if the agreement says nothing about which state's law will apply in case a question arises later about the agreement, and it is subject to interpretation by a court? In an agreement to license a database, UCITA says that the law of the licensor's state will govern.[22] Thus, under UCITA, a licensee required to impose her state's law on all contracts into which she enters will run afoul of that requirement if she accepts a database license that is silent on choice of law.[23]

Battle of the Forms

Assuming, as in most cases, that the licensor has proposed the form of the license agreement, licensors will get the last word in any battle of the forms. "If an acceptance varies from but does not materially alter the offer, a contract is formed based on the terms of the offer."[24] Interpretations of this clause will almost certainly occur in the context of litigation. To summarize what it might mean for a licensee of information, assume that the licensee receives a contract from a licensor. The licensee makes a few changes to the contract, signs it, and sends it back. If that action is interpreted as an acceptance of the contract, and if the changes are not material, they will not be part of the final agreement.

Ongoing Agreements

Another innovation of UCITA is its treatment of ongoing agreements. UCITA expressly validates agreements whose terms later change.[25] Thus, a licensor, having posted its agreement online and requiring that the licensee click "I Agree," can include a term in the agreement stating that the licensor reserves the right to unilaterally change the terms of the agreement, with no further notice of the changes. The licensee will have to check the online agreement from time to time to see if its terms have changed. So long as the link to the agreement is "conspicuous," failure to check the terms plus continued use of the licensed information may equal acceptance of the new terms.

Other surprising aspects of UCITA include the ability of licensors to disclaim warranties, even for known defects; the fact that UCITA trumps state consumer protection laws; the right of the licensor under UCITA (subject to certain conditions) to engage in "self-help" (that is, to remotely turn the licensed software or data off, making it inaccessible); and the ability to make unsuspecting licensees waive rights. Interpreting UCITA will keep lawyers in business for a long time to come.

UNIQUE OBJECT IDENTIFIERS

We expect a DOI in the long run to be able to do many
different things for many different people, far more
diverse and complex than credit cards.[26]

Enormous progress has been made in the development of persistent, unique identifiers. Among a variety of schemes, the digital object identifier (DOI) is emerging as the flagship of the online publishing community.[27] Working in concert with INDECS (Interoperability of Data in E-Commerce Systems), a consortium of international groups interested in electronic rights management and identification systems, the framers of DOI are evolving standard, effective metadata and Document Type Definition (DTD) structures, and interoperability with other schema. Because of its substantial backing in the international publishing industry, DOI is a good system to examine if one wants to grasp the portent of the online unique identifier system.

The DOI initiative will be familiar to many librarians. Those seeking information about it should consult the Web site of the International DOI Foundation (http://www.doi.org). Briefly, DOI emerged in 1997 as a project of the Association of American Publishers. Its core concept, like that of related identifier systems, is to permit the owner of any online information to tag such information, allowing seamless linking by users while maintaining owner control over the information. Key to this goal is persistence.[28] That is, unlike URLs, which may point to online information that isn't there anymore, DOIs have flexibility built in, so that the owner or location of the information can change. This is achieved through a two-part tag. Half the tag is ineluctably assigned to the information and will not change. The other half indicates the information's owner. This second half of the tag can be passed from one owner to another over time, allowing ownership, and the online location or address of the information, to change.

Publishers have registered DOIs for tens of thousands of objects, thus far mostly scholarly journal articles. The first use for the system has been reference linking among these articles.[29] Scholars with access to online research materials hail this system and already wonder how they ever lived without it. The next push is to connect sophisticated rights and permissions information, or metadata, to the DOI, which the DOI Foundation will accomplish in concert with INDECS.[30] Without the concomitant presence of permissions metadata, unique identifiers will be valueless to publishers.[31] The function of such rights metadata will be to manage the use of the digital content—who can read it, who can copy it, for what purpose, when, where. Once attached rights metadata are in place, the DOI can attain its full potential as "a digital ID for intellectual-property trading."[32]

One capability enabled by DOI is extreme granularity in the level of information identified. Not just full-length works, such as journal articles, but paragraphs and sentences within articles can be tagged, as can individual photographs or diagrams, or even single formulae.[33] Nor will the system be limited to journal articles. All content in digital form is expressed in bits and can be distributed online.[34] DOI could as easily be attached to popular music as to scholarly texts.[35] Any piece of information can be assigned an identification number. When the full capabilities of DOI and other digital identification systems are realized, and rights information is attached to each and every datum available from a publisher and every form of information or content to be had online, the Web will be overlaid with the ultimate pay-as-you-go roadmap. Users without online accounts may well be barred from this promised land.[36]

The goal of DOI is the creation of a system that will "protect customers, publishers, and rights owners."[37] Two things, however, are clear. One is that DOI is a project of the publishing community, and this community will not release information online without a system in place by which revenue can be recognized.[38] Indeed, DOI was conceived to enable "automated commercial applications."[39] The second point is that fair use is not being built into this system.[40] Is fair use a necessary casualty of the brave new world of on-demand information?

DATABASE LEGISLATION

> [W]e live in an Information Age. We should change our laws
> about who owns that information only with the greatest of care.[41]

Coverage of the recent competing congressional database protection bills has been extensive.[42] From their earlier versions to H.R. 354 and H.R. 1858, these bills have generated lively debate for a number of years.[43] No database bill has as yet been passed by Congress; however, working under the assumption that database protection legislation is inevitable, the library community supports the Bliley Bill (H.R. 1858) more than any other.

Passage of any database protection bill will represent an important directional shift in U.S. law. It is well established that U.S. copyright law does not protect facts.[44] In other words, under copyright law, facts may be copied by anyone wishing to do so.[45] Although a line of court decisions before 1991 charted a course in the protection of fact compilations, *Feist Publications, Inc. v. Rural Telephone Serv. Co.* put an end to that so-called sweat of the brow theory of protection.[46] In *Feist,* the Supreme Court announced the now settled standards for protection of groups (or compilations, or collections, now called—in the digital era— databases) of facts: (1) individual facts are not protectible, (2) at least minimal creativity is necessary to protect a collection of facts (the white pages section of a telephone directory does not meet that criterion), and (3) for protectible collections, what may not be copied are the selection, arrangement, and coordination of the facts.[47]

The current proposals do not seek to alter copyright law as it applies to facts, but rather to set up new protection, under Congress's authority to regulate commerce. The source of the law, however, will be largely irrelevant to the parties affected. The Bliley Bill is hailed by the library community as preferable to the Coble Bill (H.R. 354), because the Bliley Bill contains stronger protections for uses of data for "scientific, educational, or research" purposes. The Coble Bill, on the other hand, is seen as overly protective of the rights of database producers, and dangerously unfriendly to the library and scholarly communities.[48] The Coble Bill would penalize anyone who extracts a substantial part measured qualitatively, of a collection of information, so as to cause harm to the actual or potential market of the owner of the database.[49] The potential market need not be one that the database owner has plans to enter, but can be nothing more than a market "commonly exploited by persons offering similar products."[50] A "substantial part" defined qualitatively could be a small part of the database. Although there are some exceptions to the foregoing restrictions designed to permit the use of data for scholarly purposes, these exceptions are subject to a four-factor analysis. The extent to which research-related uses of data would be permitted under the Coble Bill is far from clear. These prohibitions would be particularly dire in the case of sole-source data, available from only one provider.

Although greatly preferable to the Coble Bill, even the Bliley Bill, if it were to pass Congress, would alter the availability of factual data for researchers and scholars. The Bliley Bill sets forth restricted activity as the distribution to the public of a duplicate of a database, in competition with that database. There are many exceptions, and there are many definitions that remain vague in the language of the bill. The "duplicate" need not be exactly the same as the original, but only "substantially" the same. "In competition" means "displaces substantial sales or licenses" of the original, and "significantly threatens the opportunity to recover a reasonable return on the investment in the collecting or organizing" of the original. Decisions by judges resolving lawsuits will be required to tell us how to define "substantial," "significant," and "reasonable return."

Excepted from the Bliley Bill are the sale of a duplicate database for scientific, educational, or research purposes, "so long as such conduct is not part of a consistent pattern engaged in for the purpose of competition" with the person or entity that collected or organized the original. Also excepted are government databases, uses of data in news reporting, and collections that have been created originally rather than by duplicating another's database.

The protections included in the Bliley Bill may prove helpful for creators of new collections of data, and for the eventual seeker of such data who might otherwise find it locked up and unavailable except for a fee. However, it is not difficult to imagine instances where uses of databases might violate rights established by the bill—distance education springs to mind.

Any database bill would change the present unprotected status of facts. Database legislation is an effort of the information industry to initiate new laws to protect commercial rights to factual information, and falls squarely within the trends outlined in this chapter.

ANTICIRCUMVENTION

> *As copyrighted works are afforded more protection, they will be encrypted in "digital wrappers" that make them impenetrable to anyone other than those who are willing to pay the going rate. While that may sound like the American way, it is not.*[51]

In the fall of 1998, Congress passed and President Clinton signed into law the Digital Millennium Copyright Act (DMCA), a monumental piece of legislation containing much that is new for practitioners in Internet Space. Those sections of the act entitled "Copyright Protection and Management Systems" (now codified at Chapter 12 of the U.S. copyright statute) are particularly important for those watching the movement toward ever-tighter control over copyrighted works. Section 1201(a)(1)(A) states: "No person shall circumvent a technological measure that effectively controls access to a work protected under this title." To "circumvent a technological measure" means "to descramble a scrambled work, to decrypt an encrypted work, or otherwise to avoid, bypass, remove, deactivate, or impair a technological measure, without the authority of the copyright owner."[52] Sections 1201(a)(2)(A) and (b)(1)(A) prohibit offering or providing products or services "primarily designed . . . for the purpose of circumventing [such] a technological measure," or the "protection afforded by [such] a technological measure." In addition, Section 1202(b) prohibits the intentional removal or alteration of any copyright management information, if there is "reasonable grounds to know, that it will induce, enable, facilitate, or conceal an infringement of any right under this title." Copyright management information includes identifying information about a work "conveyed in connection with copies . . . of a work . . . , including in digital form," such as what is set forth in a copyright notice; terms and conditions for use of a work; and "[i]dentifying numbers or symbols referring to such information or links to such information."[53] Copyright management information would undoubtedly include DOI.

The law contains an exception for a nonprofit library "which gains access to a commercially exploited copyrighted work solely in order to make a good faith determination of whether to acquire a copy of that work."[54] However, this exception applies only "when an identical copy of [the] work is not reasonably available in another form."[55]

There is no fair use exception in this law. Thus, a work that is encrypted so as to prevent access to it without the payment of a fee may not be decrypted to allow use of the work bypassing the fee requirement, even if such use would be considered unquestionably defensible under a fair use theory if brought in front of a judge. Indeed, in the first judicial decision to discuss these sections of the law, Judge Lewis Kaplan made it very clear that fair use theories do not apply to circumvention:

> Finally, defendants claim that they are engaged in a fair use under Section 107 of the Copyright Act. They are mistaken. Section 107 of the Act provides in critical part that certain uses of copyrighted works that otherwise would be wrongful are "not . . . infringement[s] of copyright." Defendants, however, are not here sued for copyright infringement. They are sued for offering to the public and providing technology primarily designed to circumvent technological measures that control access to copyrighted works and otherwise violating Section 1201(a)(2) of the Act. If Congress had meant the fair use defense to apply to such actions, it would have said so.[56]

If the DMCA applies in any given case, then whether or not a use is fair, and whether or not the applicable license agreement is enforceable, claims of infringement will simply trump all efforts to defend the use.

CONCLUSION

We're moving toward the toxic extreme of capitalism.[57]

Copyright law is giving way to technological protection, clickwrap agreements, and sui generis regimes. The ability to tag a work, or even an unprotectable fact, enclose it in a digital lockbox, and shroud it with "I Agree" license terms results in unprecedented control on the part of owners of such works or facts. The laws and initiatives discussed in this chapter as well as the recently enacted Copyright Term Extension Act (which lengthened copyright protection from life of the author plus fifty years, to life plus seventy years) are emblematic of the ever-tightening grip of ownership over content.[58] Together they constitute an arsenal of weapons against which no individual user, particularly one who can't afford license fees, is likely to prevail. Knowing these laws, and working within them to maintain the explicit Constitutional balance that preserves the public's right to know, will be the challenge of the library community.

NOTES

1. Lawrence Lessig, *Code and Other Laws of Cyberspace* (Basic Books, 1999), xi.

2. Marcie Hamilton, citing Weberian beliefs about the origins of capitalism, in *Occasional Papers in Intellectual Property from the Benjamin N. Cardozo School of Law, no. 5:* "The Historical and Philosophical Underpinnings of the Copyright Clause" at 24.

3. "I keep saying that in a time of technological flux and keen scrutiny on copyright and database legislation (and possible tightening up of users' rights in those arenas), I prefer to take my chances in the licensing environment, as we have much more control over it than over copyright." Ann Okerson, Associate University Librarian, Yale University, e-mail to author, January 19, 2000.

4. *Williams & Wilkins Co. v. United States,* 487 F.2d 1345 (Ct. Cl. 1973), aff'd by an equally divided Court, 420 U.S. 376 (1975). "Face-to-face teaching" is part of the exemption from infringement set forth in 17 USC § 110; at issue in discussions of distance education.

5. "Essential to a nuanced understanding of copyright law is the concept of commodification. By commodification, I mean the ability of a product to be distinguished from its producer. The more commodified the product, the more it is capable of traveling through a culture and its streams of commerce with value attached but independent of the identity or controlling hand of the author." Hamilton, "The Historical and Philosophical Underpinnings" at 17. "[T]his history of copyright suggests that there is an essential connection between the rise of capitalism, the extension of commodity relations into literary and artistic domains, and the emergence of the printing press." Ronald V. Bettig, *Copyrighting Culture: The Political Economy of Intellectual Property* at 9 (Westview Press, 1996).

6. Hamilton, "The Historical and Philosophical Underpinnings of the Copyright Clause," *supra* at 24.

7. Pernicious, of course, for the user community; the reader on the content owner side of the equation may wish to exploit the trend to its fullest potential.

8. Jonathan Tasini, *What Planet Are You On?: The Working Lives of Writers and the UCC2B Committee* (April 1998), http://www.2bguide.com/docs/berkjtas. html

9. The four states are Delaware, Hawaii, Illinois, and Oklahoma.

10. There are numerous articles and other texts that may be consulted on the history of UCITA and its transformation from draft Article 2B of the Uniform Commercial Code. The UCITA Online Web site (www.ucitaonline.com) and its predecessor (www.2BGuide.com) provide useful starting points.

11. See Charles Cronin, "Whither UCITA?" *AALL Spectrum,* 4, no. 4 (December 1999): 6.

12. See Report of the Committee on Copyright and Literary Property of the Association of the Bar of the City of New York on a Proposal of the National Conference of Commissioners on Uniform State Laws to Adopt a Proposed Uniform Computer Information Transactions Act, June 21, 1999; David Nimmer, Elliot Brown, and Gary N. Frischling, *The Metamorphosis of Contract into Expand,* 87 Calif. L. Rev. 17 (1999).

13. Section 105(a) of UCITA states: "A provision of this Act which is preempted by federal law is unenforceable to the extent of the preemption."

14. *ProCD, Inc. v. Zeidenberg,* 86 F.3d 1447 (7th Cir. 1996). The court enforced a shrink wrap license that placed restrictions on the use of uncopyrightable material.

15. "'Computer information' means information in electronic form which is obtained from or through the use of a computer or which is in a form capable of being processed by a computer." UCITA § 102(a)(10).

16. Opting out and opting in are permitted under section 104.

17. See generally Julie E. Cohen, *Lochner in Cyberspace: The New Economic Orthodoxy of "Rights Management,"* 97 Mich. L. Rev. 462, 481–89 (November 1998); and Mark A. Lemley, *Beyond Preemption: The Law and Policy of Intellectual Property Licensing,* 87 Calif. L. Rev. 111 (1999).

18. Although clickwraps have been upheld in a number of courts, UCITA validates and expands clickwrap practice.

19. Draft Comments to Uniform Computer Information Transactions Act § 112, note 5 (October 15, 1999).

20. UCITA § 102(a)(14); § 112.

21. UCITA §§ 112(a) and 112(e)(3).

22. A database license is called an "access contract" in UCITA § 102(a)(1).

23. Frequently, state universities require imposing their state's law on all contracts.

24. UCITA § 204(d). This is in direct contrast to standard practice under the Uniform Commercial Code. "[A]dditional terms are to be construed as proposals for addition to the contract. Between merchants such terms become part of the contract unless: (a) the offer expressly limits acceptance to the terms of the offer; (b) they materially alter it; or (c) notification of objection to them has

already been given or is given within a reasonable time after notice of them is received." UCC § 2-207(2).

25. UCITA §§ 202(b) and 208(2).

26. Norman Paskin and Godfrey Rust, *The Digital Object Identifier Initiative: Metadata Implications,* Discussion paper no. 2, Version 3 at 34 (The International DOI Foundation February 10, 1999), http://www.doi.org/P2VER3.PDF

27. Just a few of the many organizations proffering identification systems are MUZE Inc. (Entertainment Merchandise Interchange Standard), the International Federation for the Phonographic Industries (International Standard Recording Code), Book Industry Title Information Project, the International Confederation of Authors' and Composers' Societies (Common Information System), the Dublin Core Initiative, and the International Standard Audiovisual Number Initiative.

28. "If metadata is to be distributed and relied upon, an audit trail is needed to enable updates on an ongoing indefinite basis (of course, rights management requires this to a much greater extent). Metadata declared today may still be operational in twenty years time, linked to hundreds of other metadata declarations and referenced in thousands, even millions, of transactions and licences." See generally, Priscilla Caplan and William Y. Arms, "Reference Linking for Journal Articles," *D-Lib Magazine 5,* no. 7/8 (July/August 1999), http://www.dlib.org/dlib/july99/caplan/07caplan.html

29. See www.crossref.org. "Once the service is fully launched, more than three million articles across thousands of journals will be linked through CrossRef, and more than half a million more articles will be linked each year thereafter." *Journal Reference Linking Service Names Executive Director, Board of Directors, New Members, and a "Go Live" Timetable,* CrossRef press release (February 2, 2000), http://www.crossref.org/news/02022000.htm

30. See Norman Paskin, *DOI Discussion Paper: DOI Deployment* Version 2.0 (The International DOI Foundation, February 2000), http://www.doi.org/deployment2.pdf

31. "These resource mechanisms [URLs, URNs, RDF] provide an infrastructure for managing resource discovery and distribution, but not a sufficient framework in which to manage intellectual content and the rights which accompany that content, such as access rights and copyright." Norman Paskin, *The Digital Object Identifier System: Digital Technology Meets Content Management* (The International DOI Foundation, August 1998), http://www.doi.org/sun_pap2.html

32. Lloyd A. Davidson and Kimberly Douglas, "Digital Object Identifiers: Promise and Problems for Scholarly Publishing," ¶ 27, *Journal of Electronic Publishing* 4, issue 2 (December 1998), http://www.press.umich.edu/jep/04-02/davidson.html

33. A digital object can be any "*meaningful* piece of data." Paskin, *The Digital Object Identifier System.*

34. "All current varieties of intellectual property, e.g. books, music, journals, video, software, and those types yet to be invented, will be involved in this migration

[from physical to electronic dissemination], and the boundaries that exist between current content types, especially at the level of supporting infrastructure, will be eliminated." Paskin, *DOI Discussion Paper: DOI Deployment.*

35. At the October 1999 "Update on DOI" held at the Frankfurt Book Fair, it was stated that "the [International DOI] Foundation is developing the DOI as a standardised identifier for the intellectual property communities (including text, music, images, and multimedia)." Norman Paskin, *Update on Digital Object Identifier* (The International DOI Foundation, October 13, 1999), http://www.doi.org/frank_bf_oct99/oct13summary.pdf. One example metadata set in Version 3 of the International DOI Foundation's "DOI Discussion Paper Number 2" is for the CD *Graceland.* Paskin and Rust, *The Digital Object Identifier Initiative,* 45.

36. Such concerns are not lost on the library community. See Paula Berinstein, "DOI: A New Identifier for Digital Content," *Searcher* 6, no. 1 (January 1998): 72–78, http://www.infotoday.com/searcher/jan98/story4.htm; Mark Bide, "In Search of the Unicorn: The Digital Object Identifier from a User Perspective," *British National Bibliography Research Fund Report,* (Book Industry Communication, London, November 1997); and Lloyd A. Davidson and Kimberly Douglas, "Digital Object Identifiers: Promise and Problems for Scholarly Publishing," *Journal of Electronic Publishing* 4, issue 2 (December 1998): ¶ 28, http://www.press.umich.edu/jep/04-02/davidson.html

37. International DOI Foundation Web site, "About the DOI," http://www.doi.org/about_the_doi.html

38. Davidson and Douglas, "Digital Object Identifiers: Promise and Problems," ¶ 16.

39. "We will not be able to licence, sell or protect our property effectively without participating more broadly in a standardised 'network' of multi-media identifiers. This realisation was behind the conception of the DOI." Paskin and Rust, *The Digital Object Identifier Initiative,* 33.

40. Indeed, "[t]he <indecs> schema is neutral on the merits or otherwise of any given right or practice but is concerned only with the mechanisms of describing the transactions that take place." Godfrey Rust and Mark Bide, *The <indecs> Metadata Schema: Building Blocks* at section 1.5 (November 11, 1999), http://www.indecs.org/pdf/schema.pdf. INDECS rights schema identify only four possible relationships between grantors and grantees of rights, and those rights: permission, requirement, prohibition, and assignment. Id. at section 9.3.2.

41. Testimony of Jonathan Band before the U.S. House Science Committee Symposium on Database Legislation, June 17, 1999, http://www.databasedata.org/hr1858/bandsym/bandsym.html

42. See http://www.ala.org/oitp/copyright.html; http://www.arl.org/info/frn/copy/database.html; http://www.databasedata.org; http://www.infoindustry.org; and Malla Pollack, *The Right to Know?: Delimiting Database Protection at the Juncture of the Commerce Clause, the Intellectual Property Clause and the First Amendment,* 17 Cardozo Arts & Ent. L.J. 47, 61 (1999).

43. The earliest bills were H.R. 3531, introduced in 1996, and H.R. 2652, the first incarnation of Representative Howard Coble's Collections of Information Antipiracy Act. H.R. 354 is the current version of the Collections of Information Antipiracy Act, introduced in Congress in January 1999. H.R. 1858, the Consumer and Investor Access to Information Act, sponsored by Representative Thomas Bliley, was introduced in Congress in May 1999.

44. The source of this under current law is 17 U.S.C.S. 102(b): "In no case does copyright protection . . . extend to any idea, procedure, process, system, method of operation, concept, principle, or discovery. . . ."

45. Unless, that is, an entire collection of facts, or the selection or arrangement of those facts, is being copied. *Key Publications, Inc. v. Chinatown Today Publishing Enterprises, Inc.*, 945 F.2d 509, 512 (2d Cir. 1991).

46. For a succinct history of this line of reasoning, see Jane C. Ginsburg, *Statement on H.R. 2652: The Collections of Information Antipiracy Act,* submitted to the Subcommittee on Courts, Intellectual Property and the Administration of Justice of the Committee on the Judiciary (October 28, 1997), http://www.house.gov/judiciary/41147.htm. *Feist Publications, Inc. v. Rural Telephone Serv. Co.,* 499 U.S. 340 (1991).

47. *CCC Information Servs., Inc. v. Maclean Hunter Market Reports,* 44 F.3d 61 (2d Cir. 1994).

48. See commentary at http://www.databasedata.org/

49. *Collections of Information Antipiracy Act,* 106th Cong., H.R. 354, § 1402 (1999).

50. H.R. 354, 106th Cong., § 1401(3) (1999).

51. Remarks of Representative Dingell discussing the then-proposed DMCA, 144 Cong. Rec. H7099 (daily ed. Aug. 4, 1998).

52. 17 U.S.C. § 1201(a)(3)(A).

53. 17 U.S.C. § 1202(c).

54. 17 U.S.C. § 1201(d)(1). "Librarians and educators do not see much value in this provision because vendors of technically protected copyrighted works will generally have incentives to allow librarians and educators to have sufficient access to make acquisition decisions." Pamela Samuelson, *Intellectual Property and the Digital Economy: Why the Anti-Circumvention Regulations Need to Be Revised,* 14 Berkeley Technology Law Journal 519, 542 (1999).

55. 17 U.S.C. § 1201(d)(2).

56. *Universal City Studios, Inc. v. Reimerdes,* 82 F. Supp. 2d 211, 219 (S.D.N.Y. 2000). The defendant in this case was held liable for offering, via the Internet, software that enabled users to bypass the Content Scramble System, which the DVD industry uses to make certain that motion pictures on DVDs can be played but not copied.

57. Randy Komisar, co-founder of the Claris Corporation, cited in "Digital Commerce," *New York Times,* March 27, 2000, at C4.

58. *Copyright Term Extension Act,* 17 U.S.C. § 302.

8

A License to Kill For . . .

FAYE A. CHADWELL

This chapter provides a discussion of the steps necessary to create a "license to kill for." First, however, let us consider why any librarian would kill for a license. Licensing electronic journals, indeed licensing electronic resources, is not a responsibility that most collection development librarians would eagerly add to their plate. It is easier to joke that librarians might easily kill *because* of a license, having been driven to this desperate act by hierarchical and uncooperative institutional environments, unresponsive or inflexible publishers, vague or nonexistent signature authority guidelines, or indecipherable and boring legal jargon found in most terms and conditions of licensing agreements.

The truth is that librarians seek the "license to kill for" because providing dedicated, timely, and excellent service to their users demands it. Washington State University's John Webb states quite succinctly:

> There is simply no excuse for a library to accept a vendor's "standard" license agreement unless it meets all of the conditions now accepted as "best

Based on a presentation made at the Third Electronic Serials Institute, "Blazing the Trail: Electronic Serials from Acquisition to Access," April 16–17, 1999, Portland, Oregon. This material is not presented as comprehensive legal advice necessary for effectively amending and evaluating all contracts and agreements that librarians and other professionals may have with publishers and vendors. All librarians working to amend agreements are encouraged to consult with the appropriate legal advisors and to enlist their capable support in the development of licensing agreements.

109

practices" by the librarians and legal advisors to them who are the leaders in licensing issues today. It must also meet the needs of the users of the library, which must forcefully negotiate the changes necessary to make it a "win-win" agreement for both library and resource provider.[1]

Essentially then, our drive to examine licensing agreements is not out of sync with our overall mission to provide relevant research materials and deliver the best possible services to our users. Nevertheless, the process for creating that "license to kill for" may be out of sync with our traditional tasks, roles, and responsibilities as librarians. The introductory pages to Yale University's helpful Web site on licensing, titled Liblicense, state: "Licensing agreements often are complex, lengthy documents filled with arcane and unfamiliar terms such as indemnity, severability and *force majeure*."[2] In short, most librarians are not lawyers and have no immediate plans to attend law school.

Acknowledging this reality doesn't make the licensing task any less onerous, less challenging, or less significant. Rather, the exact opposite is true. Rather than stick our heads in the sand like the proverbial ostrich, we can be proud as a profession for our effective response to this new dimension to our work. Librarians have really stepped up to the plate in terms of discussing the issues, collaborating within and outside the profession, and providing education and training opportunities. The list of licensing resources included in appendix 1 at the end of this chapter provides substantial evidence of our initial and ongoing successes. It is hoped that this discussion will be a useful and engaging addition to the resources already available.

ESTABLISHING THE COLLABORATIVE ORGANIZATIONAL ENVIRONMENT

Before examining a licensing agreement in order to amend it, librarians should have in place the best possible environment for accomplishing this task. Conditions or guidelines for licensing will vary from organization to organization or from institution to institution, but across them all, librarians need to consider who should be involved, both from within and from outside the library.

External Environment

It is important to bear in mind that individuals or units from outside the library, including legal counsel, business affairs, purchasing agents, or senior administrative officers, may need to, or have to, be involved in the process. Why should librarians seek outside cooperation or consultation? For one thing, it is only right to do so because of the increased workload these individuals will face when asked to handle numerous agreements needing amendments and signatures. The chief reason to involve personnel from outside the library, however, is that librarians may not have the complete authority either to amend or to sign legally binding terms and conditions. There may be very good reasons for librarians not to have signature authority or not to be solely responsible for amending the terms of agreements. The merits of librarians having this authority, or the frustrations of not having it, should be discussed on a case-by-case basis at the individual institutional level. Until a broader discussion ensues, however, librarians should respect the boundaries of their organizational settings to avoid isolating themselves and alienating potential allies.

Once business officers or legal counsel are involved, what is the next step? Primarily, librarians need to communicate the library's needs and expectations regarding access to electronic journals. Librarians should emphasize the need for timely turnaround in completing agreements, both to avoid delaying access to essential research materials and to prevent user frustration. The turnaround time needs to be quick, particularly when a library is renewing or switching subscriptions and could lose access even for a relatively short time. Because business officers or legal counsel may not have experience or familiarity with the library's mission to provide broad, barrier-free access, it is very important that they understand that often changes or additions to the standard contractual language must be made. Overall, sharing this information should become a means of sharing expertise. Communicating expectations should present an opportunity for personnel outside the library to examine the ways that they have amended agreements in the past. Perhaps some changes will result.

Internal Environment

Within the library itself, individuals responsible for collection development, acquisitions, systems, and public services should be consulted. Some libraries organize a team or unit for managing the licensing and access of electronic resources. This team might be a short-lived task force or an ongoing committee. Whatever the composition, the goal should be to establish an efficient process for licensing, acquiring, and setting up access to electronic journals that mirrors, as much as possible, the selection and ordering of print materials.

A central contact person for all licensing issues should be selected from among the members of the library's internal working group. At first, appointing a central contact may appear to have the negative effect of slowing down the process by placing all responsibility with one person. In fact, a point person provides an easily identifiable contact for publishers, vendors, other librarians, library staff members, and personnel from outside the library as well as users. Having a central contact also prevents communication problems. Moreover, it often has the positive effects of avoiding duplication of effort and of ensuring a consistent approach to avoid unknowingly breaking the terms of an agreement.

At the University of Oregon, the internal working group includes the head of collection development, the assistant university librarian for public services and collections, and two systems librarians—the head of systems and the librarian responsible for actually setting up electronic access. In other libraries, these responsibilities might be undertaken by a single person. It is important to keep in mind why these people need to be involved. Why is their input necessary? And what will be the impact on the licensing process as well as on their departments if they are not involved?

The following example illustrates this point. After nearly a year of providing access to electronic journals at the University of Oregon, librarians realized that the acquisitions librarian could provide useful input regarding print subscriptions and contacts with serials vendors. Without this input, the head of collection development, who is the central contact for licensing at the UO libraries, would have spent her time tracking down details about print subscriptions that the acquisitions department had practically at its fingertips. Leaving the acquisitions department out of the licensing process also produced a negative effect on the workflow. Acquisitions staff were unaware of electronic journals being provided for free as part of print subscriptions, data that were crucial for updating order records and for reducing the flow of information being received from publishers and vendors about the availability of electronic access.

After members of the internal work group have been chosen, they need to complete three major tasks. First, the group should define how the term *authorized users* will be used in all agreements in the future. This important licensing issue will be discussed later in this chapter. Second, the group should develop a checklist of licensing "dos" and "don'ts" to guide its efforts to amend agreements. Such a checklist might look like the one initially developed at the University of Oregon.[3] Finally, with the definition of authorized users and the checklist in hand, the group should amend one agreement together, asking the appropriate personnel outside the library, such as legal counsel, to offer suggestions for improvement.

LICENSING ESSENTIALS

When librarians first sit down to amend an agreement, the process may seem daunting. It is important to remember two things: first, the procedure of amending a licensing agreement will remain fairly uniform over time, and, second, negotiating will become easier with every agreement as the terminology becomes familiar and the process routine.

In addition to the agreement itself, librarians should have several resources in their possession before they proceed with the amending process. Two of these resources should have been created before actually beginning work: the institutional definition of authorized users and a checklist of dos and don'ts. The third necessary resource is pricing information for the journal(s) being licensed. As they work, librarians should also consult Yale University's Liblicense Web site, working with the pages on terminology and language of contracts.

Authorized Users

The first step in actually amending an agreement is to look at how the publisher defines "authorized users." If the definition is acceptable, then no substitution or amendment to the original contract is necessary. Often, however, librarians will want to substitute their library's definition of "authorized users" (see fig. 1).

What should a good working definition of "authorized users" address? Ideally, such a definition will cover the following library users (depending on the type of library):

1. officially registered full- or part-time students of the library's institution
2. full- or part-time faculty and staff of the library's institution, including those with adjunct and courtesy appointments and active volunteers
3. community patrons who have updated public borrower cards
4. officially registered students in summer programs or institutes of the library's institution
5. authorized users of the institution's library and campus computer networks
6. authorized users at a public library defined by a geographic or service area, and limited to a single main library and its branches administered under a single director or board of trustees
7. currently enrolled students and current faculty and staff primarily affiliated with a licensed school (K–12) building or campus
8. current employees of a geographically distinct institution served by a licensed special or corporate library

The following definition refers to all license agreements between the University of XXX (as the sole licensee) and electronic journal providers/vendors:

> Authorized Users are those patrons who may have complete and unrestricted access to the content of the journal or database. The definition of Authorized Users will change in consortial agreements.

> Authorized Users refers to all those patrons who access information through terminals physically located on the site or under the control or administration of the subscribing institution.

> Authorized Users also include remote users, regardless of location or means of connection. In the case of remote access, Authorized Users are:
>> All enrolled UXXX students;
>> All current faculty and staff, including adjunct and courtesy appointments and active volunteers;
>> Community patrons with active borrowers cards;
>> Alumni Association members with activated borrowers cards;
>> President's Associates;
>> Students enrolled in special UXXX summer programs or institutes.

> Unauthorized users from remote locations include:
>> Students, faculty, staff from other educational institutions, regardless of borrowing status;
>> Community users without borrowing privileges;
>> Any other library, school, business, nonprofit, or research institution.

The UXXX will make reasonable efforts to block unauthorized access through IP address detection, controlled passwords, or other reliable and affordable security technology. New categories of Authorized Users not listed above will be negotiated with the vendor or the publisher.

FIGURE 1   Definition of an Academic Library's Authorized Users

At the very least, the definition of authorized users for academic libraries must include faculty, students, and staff and must allow for use by walk-in or on-site patrons.

When amending a publisher's definition of authorized users, librarians should strive to meet additional objectives. Librarians should emphasize that authorized users must have as complete and unrestricted access to content as is possible. Librarians must also define or address unauthorized users. Publishers need to know that librarians understand who should and should not have access to electronic journals. Also, librarians will want to pay attention to the manner in which the library or publisher will identify and authorize these users: individual registration? Individual passwords? Campuswide passwords? Use of restricted IP addresses and at what level? Some combination of these factors? Because the publisher may have concerns about who has remote access, librarians need to ensure that both parties have clearly defined the site and the locations or branches that are acceptable extensions, and they must also clarify which users have access and what authentication methods are to be employed if making use of a proxy server. Since the universe of electronic journals is constantly changing, a good definition of authorized users should be open to incorporating new categories of users. Providing such flexibility will allow librarians to extend usage to students in distance education programs, in summer programs or institutes, and in exchange programs.

Once created, a library's definition of authorized users should be included in all agreements unless the publisher's definition is palatable to all parties. However, just because a librarian produces the library world's best definition of authorized users, there is no guarantee that it will be agreeable to all publishers. If a publisher has concerns about the proposed definition, librarians and the publisher should negotiate until they concur on a mutually agreeable definition (see appendix 2, Problem 1).

Authorized Uses

In addition to determining authorized users as defined by the publisher, librarians must examine the permissible authorized uses. An overarching goal should always be to obtain the broadest type of use available. At the very least, librarians should stipulate that users must have access to materials for educational, personal, and research purposes. Some specific uses that librarians should persuade publishers to permit are:

  the right to download and store information and to what extent or for what length of time

  the right to print information and to what extent

  the right to copy information and to what extent

  the right to publish information without any expectations that users must take unrealistic steps to inform the original copyright holder

One use that more than likely will have to be negotiated is the right to interlibrary loan. Publishers' reluctance to allow interlibrary loan results directly from their anxiety about the ease with which electronic documents can be copied and distributed. Many publishers are still generally willing to allow libraries to send electronic versions of an article via interlibrary loan, if the electronic versions are first printed in hard copy. Publishers are rarely willing to permit libraries to alter, recompile, or create derivative works or to resell or redistribute the software and content of electronic journals.

Unauthorized Uses

When addressing the subject of authorized uses, librarians must also be sure to clarify who is responsible for unauthorized use(s), the steps required to prohibit it, and the consequences if unauthorized use occurs. Most librarians with licensing experience agree that librarians are no more responsible for unauthorized use of electronic journals than they are for unauthorized use of print materials. Liblicense offers this advice about librarians' responsibility for unauthorized users: Librarians should not agree "to actively police the use of licensed materials, but only to report any unauthorized use of which [they are] aware."[4] At the same time, librarians need to be willing to state in the contract that they will take reasonable steps to prohibit unauthorized use by both authorized and unauthorized users, and to keep such use from recurring.

When unauthorized use occurs, librarians have two responsibilities: to ensure that access will be maintained while addressing and correcting the violation(s), and to acknowledge that if the publisher's concerns cannot be adequately addressed, access may have to be forfeited because of breach of contract. Likewise, publishers need to understand that for most librarians, resolving problems of unauthorized use by authorized users may be easier to handle than unauthorized use by community borrowers. A university library will have stronger institutional support and guidelines in order to discipline its authorized users who violate use restrictions than it will have for handling community borrowers engaging in similar activities. Librarians in academic settings can enlist the support of faculty oversight committees, student conduct codes, and campus computing resources. Publishers must also recognize that even when an authorized user commits a violation, a library may not act on its own accord. Rather, it must follow institutional guidelines regarding library user conduct and disciplinary action.

Pricing Information

Negotiations on pricing or cost of electronic journals will probably occur before the library receives a copy of the agreement. Nevertheless, it is important to include pricing information with the amended agreement as an attachment, if a place for pricing information is not provided. An organization's legal counsel or business office may require this information. Many states and cities have regulations about handling purchases in certain price ranges and about who must sign an agreement when the price is above a specific amount. In general, it is safe to say that price may dictate willingness or ability to be flexible on the part of a library's parent institution or organization.

In addition to including the cost of electronic journals, it is imperative to present the pricing model and the basis for setting the price. In some cases, librarians will receive a separate accompanying document, often called a subscription or order form, outlining the costs, if any, and requesting that such items as IP addresses, related print subscriptions, and library contacts be provided (see fig. 2).

American Society for Educational Excellence
Subscription Form
Customer Services, PO Box 002, New York, NY 00002,
phone: 212-222-2222, 212-122-2222

Subscriber name: <u>University of the Northwest</u>
Address: <u>1333 University of the Northwest</u>
                     <u>Sisters, OR</u>
Contact Person: <u>Jane Librarian</u>
Phone: <u>503-111-1111</u>   Fax: <u>503-111-1110</u>
Email: <u>janelibrarian@un.unorthwest.edu</u>

Subscribing to Print: Online   Print+
                                           Only   Online

Journal of Educational Excellence A
Journal of Educational Excellence B
Journal of Educational Excellence C
Journal of Educational Excellence D

Purchase Order Number: <u>585855</u>
Institution's IP Address(es):   <u>888.888*</u>

Please read and sign the attached Terms and Conditions. By signing below you certify that you have read and agree to abide by all such Terms and Conditions.

Authorized signature: _____

Title of authorized signer (please print): _____

FIGURE 2   Pricing Information

The pricing models for electronic journals can and will vary; librarians may have the option of obtaining electronic access because their libraries subscribe to the print version of a title, of obtaining electronic access only, or of acquiring a package deal for electronic access to all a publisher's titles even if the library does not subscribe to the print version of those titles. Publishers may also base pricing on a variety or combination of factors: the size of the user community, the size of the materials budget, the actual recorded use of the product, or the level and the degree of access. To determine the size of the user community, the publisher may consider the full-time equivalent (FTE) for the entire user community or the FTE for particular departments. As for actual recorded use, publishers may consider unlimited simultaneous use; a specified number of users, perhaps within a particular building or set of buildings; or the number of actual transactions. Publishers may offer licenses for an entire site, at either the class B or the class C level; for a specified number of subnets; or for a specified number or set of terminals. It is worthwhile to note that more librarians will be acquiring electronic journal access through consortial deals and, as a result, we can expect pricing models and definitions of FTE, along with other licensing factors, to become more complicated.

CONTRACT ELEMENTS

Standard elements found in most contracts cover the following issues: contract renewal; transfer, breach, and termination of an agreement; warranty or guarantee (basically a performance check); liability; indemnification; *force majeure;* governance; severability; and what constitutes the complete and entire agreement. Although these elements rarely differ from one agreement to the next, librarians should still be cautious about them. These items may seem boilerplate, yet may prove to be the most challenging. Therefore, most librarians might need more assistance in amending these sections of agreements, because of their unfamiliarity with the relevant laws and guidelines governing such issues as liability, indemnification, and governing clauses.

Contract Renewal

Almost every agreement contains a clause covering the renewal of the contract or licensing agreement. In most cases, this clause will provide for automatic renewal of a subscription. If not, it will stipulate that the librarian must notify the publisher before the contract ends, should the library no longer wish to subscribe to a title. In most cases, this clause will stipulate the number of days before the expiration of the contract (typically five, thirty, or ninety days) by which the librarian must notify the publisher of the intention to cancel the subscription. The librarian must decide if the allotted time is reasonable and, if not, consider changing it.

Transfer of Assignment, Breach, and Termination

Contractual elements that occur with as much frequency as contract renewal cover transfer of assignment, breach, and termination. Most often these clauses are written to provide greater benefit to the publisher than to the library. For example, the publisher has the right to transfer the assignment of the contract to another party if the publisher sells its company to another firm, or if it buys a smaller company to administer its contract and sell its products. The publisher also usually gives itself the right to terminate an agreement if the library breaches any terms of the contract.

As much as possible, librarians should attempt to achieve reciprocity on these issues. Especially in regard to breach and termination, librarians should attempt to establish a situation in which termination is not automatic upon breach of contract. Instead, if a breach occurs, librarians should have an opportunity to correct the problem in a reasonable amount of time—whatever that might be—before termination of access and of the contract result. Librarians should also be aware that publishers may stipulate that, in addition to seeking termination of a contract because of a breach, they will pursue other legal rights and remedies. Librarians must ask what these rights and remedies are, and, before agreeing to them, consider how they might violate state laws and regulations or users' rights.

Warranty

The warranty statement of most agreements will indicate that electronic journals are provided on an "as is" basis. This means that the publisher will not provide any kind of warranty. A warranty details what to expect from a product in terms of:

    level of service
    accuracy of information
    absence of malfunction or defects
    applicability of use
    violation of someone else's intellectual property rights

Although it is unlikely that most librarians will be able to amend such guarantees successfully, it is still prudent to consider stipulating that if the level or delivery of service should fail for a specific period, the library will have some recourse and may take either of the following actions: (1) terminate the access and the contract or (2) receive a partial or full reimbursement. Librarians may even devise a standard statement to include in all licensing agreements (see appendix 2, Problem 2). Including such a stipulation is especially important when libraries are paying for access to a product, when the service loss is the publisher's fault (rather than because of *force majeure*), or when reconnection to the resources is not immediately forthcoming.

Liability

Liability generally goes hand in hand with warranty. Usually, publishers do not want to accept responsibility for exemplary, special, indirect, incidental, or consequential damages. For most librarians, this level of liability is reasonable and acceptable. When publishers do not want to accept responsibility for direct damages, however, librarians should consider automatically amending the agreement to eliminate the term *direct*.

Regarding issues of liability, librarians must also be aware of how a particular agreement addresses not only the type of damages, such as special, indirect, or consequential, but also the amount of damages a publisher is willing to pay. The tremendously resourceful Liblicense Web site does an impressive job of outlining the limitations of liability:

> In addition to making (no) promises and stating who will pay for certain costs if they arise, many agreements address the amount and kind of damages the licensor will pay. If some claim or cause of action actually gets through the first line of defense (disclaiming all warranties), the licensor may further limit its liability by providing: a monetary cap on damages, that certain kinds of damages are excluded (special, incidental, consequential), that certain harms are excluded (harms resulting from defects in, unavailability or use of the software or data).[5]

Librarians would do well to consider any and all limitations on liability and any restrictions on types of damages or monetary caps. Otherwise, they risk losing more than just access to electronic journals. They risk losing subscription fees and unknowingly limiting the amount of damages to which an injured party (including their own organization) might legitimately have claim.

Indemnification

Indemnification also relates to warranty and liability. An indemnity clause establishes who will be responsible for costs should problems or difficulties develop. For the most part, librarians should assume that the publisher will bear the cost of handling any problems that occur, especially if the problems are not caused by the library. Otherwise, librarians should beware of agreements that stipulate that they should pay for these costs (see appendix 2, Problem 3). Librarians also need to be aware of possible limitations on the indemnity clause that the library's institution or governing body will not allow under law.

Force Majeure

A *force majeure* (greater force) clause acknowledges that events beyond the control of the publisher, such as natural disasters, "Acts of God," war, or third-party failure, do happen and may hinder the availability of a product. These clauses are meant to excuse the consequences of such an event when it is truly beyond the control of the publisher. It is not meant to excuse them because they were not exercising care in judgment (see appendix 2, Problem 2).

Governance

A governance clause determines what state's or country's laws will govern the terms and conditions of an agreement. It also establishes which state's or country's courts will be the source for arbitrating any and all potential lawsuits. For most academic and public libraries, the governance clause will reflect the law(s) of the state in which the library is located. Librarians should recognize that it is advantageous to their local lawyers to be able to argue a case in a court where they are most familiar with the laws and regulations. For the most part, publishers are agreeable to amendments to this clause or even to deleting it altogether.

Severability

A severability clause establishes that if one particular term or condition within an agreement is proven invalid or is not enforceable, the rest of the contract remains valid.

Complete and Entire Agreement

When amending a contract, it is important to pay attention to any statements about what constitutes the "complete and entire agreement." Most of the time, this statement suggests that all terms and conditions are set down within the written contract rather than through any verbal negotiations. It can also clarify that the written contract and any accompanying addenda will be the record of negotiations.

SERVICE ISSUES

When negotiating licenses for electronic journals, librarians must pay attention to language regarding services to be provided, including usage statistics, compatibility, and technical assistance.

Provision of Usage Statistics

Negotiating for the provision of usage statistics may prove to be the most important activity that collection development librarians will undertake regarding renewal and future use of electronic journals. Whether libraries actually pay for access to electronic journals or just add access to a print subscription, libraries still pay for the time and effort that staff members spend identifying, selecting, licensing, setting up access to, and cataloging electronic journals. Librarians need to be sure that the staff time and energy are well spent, and that users are making the most of the product, and they should attempt to obtain usage statistics when negotiating and amending a licensing agreement. Simply adding the following statement might at least trigger a conversation between the publisher and the library about why usage statistics are important:

> Publisher X will provide Licensee with quarterly usage reports. Each report will provide the number of sessions or number of transactions by month for the Licensee.

Compatibility and Related Issues

Although the Y2K scare is behind us, librarians need to be sure that publishers of electronic resources are equipped and are preparing for new developments in technology. Also, publishers need to inform librarians of any plans they may have regarding browser capability, compatibility with lower versions of the browser, formats for providing copies of documents or articles such as PDF, technology for archiving issues, and new means of authorizing users. The stability of the URL is also a basic concern for librarians creating Web pages and cataloging Web resources. To protect against troublesome changes, librarians might opt to include in the agreement a statement such as:

> Publisher will take reasonable steps to ensure that the Library has continuous access to its electronic journals, that routine updates will not disrupt the usage of materials, and that performance of the Product will remain as effective as similar databases being offered to similar users.

Technical Assistance

Most often, if technical assistance is mentioned at all in an agreement, it will simply be a statement noting that assistance is available and specifying the dates and times for this assistance. Technical assistance is frequently not included, because publishers may not be as used to dealing directly with librarians as are vendors for databases, serials, and books (see appendix 2, Problem 4). Nevertheless, such inexperience on the part of publishers makes a strong case for adding the information about technical assistance rather than excluding it. Likewise, librarians should expect an appropriate level of technical assistance for resources that they license and acquire.

MANAGEMENT ISSUES

Librarians might believe they are naturally inclined to managing and retrieving information well. Unfortunately, this may not always be the case when dealing with documents that have been created as part of their daily work. When handling licensing agreements for a group of electronic journals, it is especially important to document all the processes and steps involved. Librarians should keep copies of all the various drafts or the extra paperwork or computer documents created as a result of amending and adding information to a publisher's pre-existing licensing agreement. Only when the access is provided should the librarian consider recycling some of the paperwork. Here are some tips for developing amendments or addenda to licensing agreements:

> Compose the amendments or changes using word-processing documents, labeled so that it is easy to identify the amendments for a particular publisher's agreement. Maintain a central file to make it easy to cut and paste certain statements regarding governance, authorized users, and so on that librarians regularly change in all agreements. Such a file allows for consistency of terminology and changes across all amended agreements.

> Print three copies of the agreement—two for the publisher to sign and one for the library.

> Combat publishers' reluctance to return a copy of the signed licensing agreement by writing a standard letter to accompany all amended agreements. This letter should state firmly and politely that one of the signed copies must be returned to the library in order for the agreement to take effect.

Here are some tips for organizing and maintaining files of agreements:

Create and maintain files of agreements based on where they fall in the licensing process. These might include such distinctions as: (1) licenses to be amended; (2) licenses that are amended, but waiting for signature from either the appropriate signature authority or from the publisher; and (3) signed and fully executed agreements that have established access.

Develop databases using such software as Microsoft Access to manage the terms and conditions as they vary on a per-publisher, per-contract basis. These terms might include information about rights to ILL, printing, downloading, and user restrictions as well as basic access information, such as password and the proper level of access. Creating a database would work well for a single-librarian operation or within a large library where the responsibilities are shared across departments and divisions. Depending on the type of integrated library systems they use, librarians may also be able to put some important information about electronic access in the catalog record for the title.

Make this database available via an Intranet or restricted server so that more librarians can check on the terms and on the bargaining status of agreements.

CONCLUSION

The availability of licensing resources on the Web and in the professional literature and the sharing of expertise via electronic discussion lists have grown tremendously during the past decade. Every librarian should take advantage of these resources because they will make the negotiation of licensing agreements much easier. Excellent local, regional, and even national institutes and workshops are available that provide opportunities for learning about new issues and offer first-rate training in or orientation to this new aspect of librarians' responsibilities. These resources can help librarians continue to provide the best possible access to information.

NOTES

1. John Webb, "Managing Licensed Networked Electronic Resources in a University Library," *Information Technology and Libraries* 17, no. 4 (December 1998): 199.
2. See: http://www.library.yale.edu/~llicense/intro.shtml, ¶ 3.

3. See: http://darkwing.uoregon.edu/~chadwelf/checlist.htm
4. See: http://www.library.yale.edu/~llicense/usecls.shtml, "Consequences of Unauthorized Use."
5. See: http://www.library.yale.edu/~llicense/warrgen.shtml

APPENDIX 1
Licensing Resources

Licensing Resources from Yale University

LIBLICENSE: Licensing Digital Information, A Resource for Librarians
http://www.library.yale.edu/~llicense/index.shtml

LIBLICENSE-on liblicense-l@lists.yale.edu Subscribe to this electronic discussion list at:
http://www.library.yale.edu/~llicense/mailing-list.shtml

Licensing Resources from the Association of Research Libraries

ARL E JOURNAL ELECTRONIC DISCUSSION LIST—Information available at:
http://www.cni.org/Hforums/arl-ejournal/about.html

Electronic discussion list subscription link at:
http://www.cni.org/Hforums/arl-ejournal/

ARL booklet: Licensing Electronic Resources: Strategic and Practical Considerations for Signing Electronic Information Delivery Agreements
http://www.arl.org/scomm/licensing/licbooklet.html

Additional Licensing Resources
International Coalition of Library Consortia's Statement of Current Perspective and Preferred Practices for the Selection and Purchase of Electronic Information
http://www.library.yale.edu/consortia/statement.html

Principles for Licensing Electronic Resources developed by several library associations, including the American Library Association, the Special Libraries Association, and the American Association of Law Librarians
http://www.arl.org/scomm/licensing/principles.html

Samples of Model Standard Licenses, a site sponsored by and developed in close cooperation with five major subscription agents: Blackwell, Rowecom, EBSCO, Harrassowitz, and Swets
   http://www.licensingmodels.com

University of Oregon Libraries—A Checklist for Negotiating Licensing Agreements
   http://darkwing.uoregon.edu/~chadwelf/checlist.htm

APPENDIX 2
Problems

Problem 1

A licensing agreement includes the following language about authorized users:

> For purposes of this Agreement, "AUTHORIZED USERS" means only the employees, faculty, staff, and students officially affiliated with the SUBSCRIBER.

What are some possible revisions that might broaden the scope of authorized users as defined in this statement?

(1) Add the category of walk-in or on-site patrons to the list.
(2) Substitute the entire definition of "AUTHORIZED USERS" with a library's predetermined and more inclusive definition (see fig. 2).

Problem 2

A licensing agreement includes the following language addressing breach of contract, warranty, and *force majeure:*

> Either party's failure to perform any term or condition of this Agreement as a result of condition beyond its control such as, but not limited to, war, strikes, floods, governmental restrictions, power failures, or damage or destruction of any network facilities or services, shall not be deemed a breach of this Agreement. However,

> *should any event outlined above continue for a period*
> *in excess of 30 days either party shall be entitled to ter-*
> *minate this Agreement by written notice to the other*
> *party.*

What are some possible revisions to this statement that might offer a library additional benefits or safeguards as a result of its potential loss of access to this resource?

(1) Add a statement specifying that in the event of termination, the publisher shall refund the library a pro rata portion of the license fees paid to the publisher.

(2) Add a statement stipulating that: "In the event that through the fault of Licensor, the Licensee is unable to access the Licensed Material for more than XX (XX) hours in total during any month of this Agreement, the Licensor shall refund to Licensee a pro rata portion of the license fees paid to the Licensor for each hour over XX (XX) hours per month that the Licensed Material is unavailable."

Problem 3

A licensing agreement includes the following language about responsibility for unauthorized use, responsibility for the activities of authorized users, and indemnification:

> *The Subscriber assumes sole responsibility for all use of*
> *the Publisher's online journals by the Subscriber and each*
> *Authorized User. In the event of a breach of this Agree-*
> *ment by the Subscriber or Authorized Users, the Sub-*
> *scriber agrees to indemnify and hold the Publisher*
> *harmless from and against any and all claims, liabilities,*
> *damages, expenses including attorneys' fees and experts'*
> *costs, penalties, and fees, if any, for the enforcement of*
> *this Agreement and otherwise for the Publisher's defense*
> *of indemnified claims, losses, and threatened losses aris-*
> *ing from or in connection with that breach, including*
> *without limitation, claims of unauthorized use.*

What are some possible revisions to this paragraph that might prevent the library from taking responsibility for unauthorized use, even by an authorized user?

(1) Change the first statement to read that the Subscriber only assumes responsibility for use of the journals by the Subscriber.

(2) Amend the second statement likewise, deleting the reference to authorized users.

(3) Add any necessary provisions from state law or regulations of appropriate governmental bodies that would decrease the Subscriber's level of liability for the losses.

Problem 4

A licensing agreement includes the following language about customer support:

> *Any assistance via telephone that Company X may provide to the Subscriber is provided at the sole risk of the Subscriber.*

How might a librarian address such a statement about customer support?

(1) Rewrite the statement to specify that technical assistance is provided on certain days of the week at specified times, and provide the appropriate contact information.

(2) Delete the statement.

9

Cataloging Electronic Resources
The Practicalities

NORMA J. FAIR AND STEVEN C. SHADLE,
WITH AN INTRODUCTION BY BEVERLEY GEER

When I was in college, I had an English literature professor who said something I've never forgotten: "Life is just one damn thing after another." The context of his statement was our study of Dante, but not a week goes by that I don't find myself saying those same words to myself. Every day in this modern world where I live and breathe brings something new, astonishing, wonderful, terrible, and, best of all, challenging. As a cataloger, especially as a serials cataloger, I've developed my own version of my professor's words: Cataloging is just one damn new thing after another. When I began my cataloging career, microformats were the new challenge for libraries. We asked ourselves: How do we house them? How do we provide physical access? Should we catalog them? I can imagine that at the turn of the twentieth century, librarians everywhere went through similar discussions about sound recordings. Look around your library now. Wouldn't you call those materials commonplace? How did we solve the problems and answer the questions surrounding sound recordings and microformats? We did not ignore them, and we could not choose to omit them from our col-

Based on presentations made at the Second Electronic Serials Institute, "Under the Arch: Electronic Serials from Acquisition to Access," April 24–25, 1998, St. Louis, Missouri, and the Third Electronic Serials Institute, "Blazing the Trail: Electronic Serials from Acquisition to Access," April 16–17, 1999, Portland, Oregon.

lections and deny library users access to them. Those options were not available, not even considered (well, maybe for a minute or two). Instead, we took a deep breath and met the challenge. We took the time-honored tools and concepts used to acquire, describe, organize, and provide access to print resources, revised them, and applied them.

The purpose of this chapter is to provide a brief overview of current cataloging procedures for electronic resources, primarily electronic journals, with the caveat that the standards and practices may change in the future. The sections that follow provide a concise, level-headed, and understandable discussion of practices involving electronic resources. These guidelines are based on rules and conventions that are clearly stated in the cataloging code and utilized by catalogers around the world. To begin, the entire process is brought into focus by a review of our oldest and most basic rules and concepts—those established by Charles Cutter many years ago. So yes, serials cataloging is one damn thing after another, but wouldn't life be boring if it were not that way?

CUTTER'S CONTEXT

Charles Cutter outlined the following purposes of a library catalog: (1) to enable a person to find a book if either the author, the title, or the subject is known; (2) to show what the library has by a given author, on a given subject, or in a given kind of literature; and (3) to assist in the choice of a book as to its edition (bibliographically) or its character (literary or topical).[1] With the Internet burgeoning with electronic resources, Cutter's principles are being applied to create traditional bibliographic records that inform users about remote electronic resources to which a library subscribes or that are in the public domain. As an added value, the catalog record for an electronic resource can lead the user directly to the content of the material via the electronic address.

APPLYING EXISTING CONVENTIONS

Landmarks for both electronic resources and their bibliographic descriptions are fluid. Although electronic journals based on print resources, such as those supplied by JSTOR and Project Muse, are relatively stable, many Internet resources are prone to change. The presentation of the title in the electronic resource may vary from one viewing to the next; content or coverage may vary; the electronic location or method of access may change; or the resource itself may cease to exist. In addition, the nature of Internet publishing is such that an electronic journal is often organized differently than a print journal (in distributed files or databases) and doesn't follow the same standards for display of bibliographic information, thus making it difficult to apply existing serials cataloging conventions to electronic journals.

BIBLIOGRAPHIC DESCRIPTION

Currently, bibliographic descriptions of electronic serials are constructed according to AACR2R chapters 1, 9, and 12, in conjunction with the *Library of Congress Rule Interpretations* (LCRI) for those chapters, and the MARC21 Format. Further guidelines are available in *Cataloging Internet Resources: A Manual and Practical Guide* (Olson), *CONSER Cataloging Manual, Module 31: Remote Access Computer File Serials*, and other resources listed under Standards and Guidelines in appendix 1. However, these standards and guidelines are fluid. Proposals being presented to the Joint Steering Committee for Revision of AACR may result in revisions to the rules for the description of serials and other ongoing publications, including electronic resources.

Is It a Serial?

The AACR2R definition of a serial applies to electronic serials: "A publication issued in successive parts bearing numeric or chronological designations and intended to be continued indefinitely."[2] The requirement for successive parts bearing numeric or chronological designation requires the cataloger to consider many electronic journals as monographs, or, more specifically, online loose-leafs that have updated material but lack issue designation. Applying this definition to electronic serials has the unfortunate result that the print versions of some journal titles will be cataloged serially, but the online versions of those same titles will be cataloged monographically.

Where Do I Look?

According to AACR2R, the chief source of information for an electronic resource is the title screen. For an electronic serial, it is the title screen of the first or earliest issue. Unfortunately, like the title page of a print serial, most electronic journals don't have a clearly defined title screen associated with the first or earliest issue, but, instead, have formal presentations on other sources, such as the journal home page; the source document metadata; "about," "readme," or "publisher's statement" pages; current issue or volume contents page; or links from other resources. After choosing the chief source or chief source substitute from which to transcribe title and edition statement (AACR Area 1 and 2), any other sources within the electronic resource or information from external sources may be used to complete the bibliographic description.

SEPARATE RECORDS VERSUS SINGLE RECORDS

AACR2R Rule 0.24 cites as a "cardinal principle" that the bibliographic description is based on the physical carrier, and, thus, a separate record is created in order that the electronic nature of an online resource can be described. In practice, many libraries follow the CONSER guidelines that allow the option of noting the existence and online location of an electronic version on the bibliographic record for the print version. A single record may be used if the electronic version has substantially the same content as the print version and, according to cataloger judgment, may be used as a reasonable substitute for the print version. A separate record is required if the electronic resource is available only online, or if the print version ceases and it is continued only online. Examples of single and separate record approaches may be found in appendix 2.

Separate Record Approach

Leader/06 (Type of record)

With the completion of format integration in 1996, all bibliographic records for electronic serials in OCLC were converted to Type code "m" (computer file format). But a new definition of Type code "m" approved by MARBI in June 1997 and implemented in early 1998 limits the use of the computer file format to certain categories of computer files, namely: software, numeric data, computer-oriented multimedia, and online systems and services. Other types of computer files are cataloged using the format for the most significant aspect of the material. Most electronic journals are primarily textual materials and are currently cataloged using the Type "a" format. Guidelines issued before March 1998, as well as many older OCLC bibliographic records, reflect the earlier practice.

MARC21 006/007/008

006 Additional material characteristics

When the Type code does not equal "m," code the 006 field to represent the computer file aspects of the resource. Conversely, if the Type code equals "m," code the 006 field for the serial aspects of the resource.

007 Physical Description Fixed Field

Code the 007 for the computer file characteristics. Typical 007 field for Internet resources:

> 007 $a c $b r $d c $e n $f u
>
> $a   Category of material c = computer file
>
> $b   Specific material designation r = remote
>
> $d   Color c = multicolored
>
> $e   Dimensions n = not applicable
>
> $f   Sound u = unknown

008 Fixed length data elements

Use the serial 008 (Type *a*, Bib Level *s*) for serially issued textual electronic resources.

Uniform Title and Title Proper

130 Uniform Title (LCRI 25.5B)

If the computer file serial is also issued in another physical format, use a uniform title with a qualifier for the physical medium, for example (Online).

> 130 0   Administrative science quarterly (Online)
>
> 130 0   Development (Cambridge, England : Online)

245 Title proper and general material designation (GMD) (AACR2R 1.1.C1)

Use subfield $h [computer file] immediately after the title proper.

> 245 00 Administrative science quarterly $h [computer file]

Physical Description

300 Physical Description

An online resource has no physical characteristics. Do not use field 300 for remote access resources.

Notes and Linking Fields

506 Restrictions on access note (AACR2R 9.7B20)

A 506 note may be used when the publication is not freely available and the electronic location is given in the 856 field. In a local system, it may be preferable to give restrictions on access in the 856 subfield $z, public note, as it may be more prominently displayed there.

506	Access limited to users with <institution> IP addresses.
506	Password available at Documents Reference Desk.
506	Access restricted to institutions with a print subscription and requires a site/user ID and password.

516 Type of computer file or data note (AACR2R 9.B1)

Make a note if the computer file characteristics are not otherwise clear in the record.

516	Numeric (Summary statistics).
516	Text (Law reports and digests).
516	Hypertext (Electronic journal).
516	Available in ASCII, Acrobat, and PostScript file formats.

530 Other physical formats available (AACR2R 9.7B16)

Describe the existence of other format(s). Cite the related bibliographic record(s) in linking field 776 (Additional physical form entry).

530	Online version of print publication.
530	Also issued in print version.

538 Mode of access note (AACR2R 9.7B1c)

Provide a note to explain the means by which the serial can be accessed.

538	Mode of access: Internet.
538	Available electronically via Internet.
538	Mode of access: World Wide Web via Internet.

538 System requirements note (AACR2R 9.7B1a)

Make "system requirements" notes for *special* software, equipment, or operating systems required to capture or print the electronic file.

> 538   System requirements: Adobe Acrobat to view full text of articles in PDF file format.

776 Additional physical form entry

Add a 776 linking field for the print version, if applicable.

> 776 1 $t Development (Cambridge, England) $x 0950-1991 $w (DLC) 89655551 $w (OcoLC)15088415

Electronic Location and Access

856 Electronic location and access

Give the electronic address of the item as well as the information needed to access the item.

> 856 50 $u http://www.biologists.com/Development/
>
> 856 40 $u http://agebb.missouri.edu/agforest/archives/

Single Record Approach

If the electronic resource is determined to be essentially the same as the print version of the same title, the existence and location of the electronic version may be noted on the bibliographic record for the print version by adding the following fields to the print version record:

007 Physical description fixed field

Optionally, add field 007 for the remote computer file characteristics.

530 Note the availability of the online version in field 530 (AACR2R 12.7B16)

> 530   Backfile also issued online via JSTOR.
>
> 530   Also available to subscribers in online version.

740 Make a 740 title added entry for the title of the electronic version if it differs from the print version.

776 If a separate ISSN has been assigned to the online serial but a separate record doesn't exist, add field 776 with subfields $t and $x.

856 Electronic location and access

Give the electronic address for the remote resource.

> 856 41 $u http://agebb.missouri.edu/agforest/archives/
>
> 856 41 $u http://www.biologists.com/Development/

SUBJECT ANALYSIS/GENRE HEADINGS

According to David Haykin, "Form subdivision may be defined as the extension of a subject heading based on the form or arrangements of the subject matter in the book. In other words, it represents what the book is, rather than what it is about, the subject matter being expressed by the main heading."[3]

The assignment of subject headings for electronic serials is very similar to that for print serials. *Library of Congress Subject Headings* (LCSH) provide no standard form or genre subdivision for electronic resources. In fact, the instructions in the *Subject Cataloging Manual: Subject Headings* (H1580.5) direct the cataloger to use the subdivision—*Periodicals* for electronic serials. The assumption is that the electronic nature of a journal does not inherently make an e-journal a distinct bibliographic form, and the bibliographic description, as created using AACR2R and MARC21, is sufficient to convey the "e" nature of these resources. The editors of *Medical Subject Headings* (MeSH) have established *Electronic journals* as a form subheading for "periodicals published and distributed electronically."

Libraries that identify electronic journals as one of Cutter's "editions" and wish to assist the user in identifying e-journals are not able to do so easily within the environment of national-level current cataloging standards. Several leaders in the cataloging community have proposed that catalogs take advantage of MARC21, 007 Physical Description Fixed Field, to indicate the remote nature of a computer file. Thus, the combination of the fixed field (007 $a c $b r) with some other field that indicates "journalness" (for example, 650 $x Periodicals or Bib Lvl s) can be used by online systems to identify these resources for the user. Unfortunately, very few libraries have online catalogs that actually make use of this field as a limiting device in the public interface. Instead, libraries have identified a wide variety of other strategies that have been used for identification or retrieval of electronic journals.[4]

One of the most common methods to provide this access, for those libraries not using MeSH, is to assign a local, genre heading to their e-journals. The MERLIN libraries in Missouri chose to use the following genre heading to enable a search limit in the OPAC for electronic resources.[5] The term used for electronic journals is the LCSH term "Electronic journals," resulting in the genre heading:

655 #7 Electronic journals. $2 lcsh

Other commonly used genre terms added to electronic resource records include:

655 #7 Computer network resources. $2 lcsh

655 #7 Electronic newspapers. $2 lcsh

Instead of adding a separate genre term, some libraries have also adopted MeSH practice with LC subject headings by replacing—*Periodicals* with—*Electronic journals.*

CLASSIFICATION

Applying library classification to electronic journals also raises questions. In North American libraries, classification of journals is not a standard practice by any means, and as many libraries shelve their collections by title as by classification. However, some libraries have used call numbers as an identification or retrieval mechanism by assigning a generic (for example, EJOURNAL, Electronic Journal, Internet) or specific (Project Muse) phrase as the call number. Other libraries have transcribed the URL in the place of the call number. Some libraries have also used a standard cutter appended to the classification number to identify Internet resources, thus collocating electronic and nonelectronic resources in the catalog.

Other libraries and library-related projects have taken advantage of classification to support subject collocation and retrieval in Web-based collections.[6]

HOLDINGS

Libraries use various methods to indicate holdings information for electronic journals. Some libraries use a summary statement in a holdings record, similar to treatment for tangible materials; others refer users to a library Web page or the journal Web site for coverage information. Because of the ease with which users can connect to resources through a Web-based catalog—one click away—and the fact that holdings can change without the knowledge of the library, some libraries simply provide a generic note rather than attempting to provide detailed holdings information.

When holdings information is made available, a common practice is to give coverage information in subfield $z (public note) of the 856 field, thus displaying both the holdings and the link with the hope that the user will actually read the holdings statement before going to the e-journal. The MERLIN libraries use the $z technique, listing the "holding" library symbol(s) and coverage statement for available resources. MERLIN libraries use no subfield $z for resources in the public domain.

> 856 41 $z MU, UMK have: v.39(1996)- $ u http://www.ref.
> oclc.org:2000/journal=0964-0568

> 856 41 $z MU, SLU have: v.1(1892)- Latest 3 years not
> available online. $u http://www.jstor.org/journals/
> 00308108.html

CONCLUSION

Now don't you feel better? Don't you feel prepared for the challenge? Or have you read (and I suggest that you do so lest you become too comfortable) Regina Romano Reynolds's chapter entitled "Seriality and the Web"? If you have, then you read such phrases as "unresolved issues," "out-of-control," and "proliferate" alongside "evolution," "encouraging," and "plan for a new future." People like Regina and the other contributors to this book have interesting things to say about the future of serials. What is common among them is that they use the word "challenge" in a positive way. You can go away from all you read here agreeing with me that cataloging, especially serials cataloging, is one damn thing after another, but please don't say it or think it in a discouraged way. Instead, say what my grandmother would say when faced with a challenge, with something new and interesting: "Well, that beats anything I ever stepped in."

NOTES

1. Charles A. Cutter, *Rules for a Dictionary Catalog,* 4th ed. (Washington, D.C.: Government Printing Office, 1904), 12.

2. *Anglo-American Cataloguing Rules,* 2nd ed., 1998 revision (Chicago: American Library Association, 1998), 622.

3. David Judson Haykin, *Subject Headings: A Practical Guide* (Washington, D.C.: Government Printing Office, 1951).

4. Steve Shadle, "Identification of Electronic Journals in the Online Catalog," *Serials Review* 24, no. 2 (summer 1998): 104–107.

5. *Cataloging Standards and Guidelines for Use in Maintaining the MERLIN Library Catalog,* 8.2. Electronic Resources. See: http://merlin.missouri.edu/lso/standard/080201_808202_Electronic_Res_BW.htm

6. Traugott Koch, et al., *The Role of Classification Schemes in Internet Resource Description and Discovery* (Bath: UK Office for Library and Information Networking, 1997). See: http://www.ukoln.ac.uk/metadata/desire/classification/; Gerry McKiernan, *Cyberstacks(sm)* (Ames: Iowa State University, 1996–). See: http://www.public.iastate.edu/~CYBERSTACKS; and Steve Shadle and Alex Wade, *Putting It All Together: The Involvement of Technical Services, Public Services and Systems to Create a Web-based Resource Collection* (Seattle: University of Washington Libraries, 1999). See: http://www.lib.washington.edu/about/registry/nasig/

APPENDIX 1
Standards and Guidelines

Anglo-American Cataloguing Rules. 2nd ed., 1998 revision. Chicago: American Library Association, 1998.

Beck, Melissa. *CONSER Cataloging Manual, Module 31: Remote Access Computer File Serials.* Revised September 10, 1999. See: http://lcweb.loc.gov/acq/conser/module31.html

Guidelines for Coding Electronic Resources in Leader/06. Network Development and MARC Standards Office, Library of Congress. See: http://lcweb.loc.gov/marc/ldr06guide.html

Guidelines for the Use of Field 856. Revised August 1999. Prepared by Network Development and MARC Standards Office, Library of Congress. See: http://www.loc.gov/marc/856guide.html

MARC21 Format for Bibliographic Data: Including Guidelines for Content Designation. Prepared by Network Development and MARC Standards Office, Library of Congress, in cooperation with Standards and Support, National Library of Canada. Washington, D.C.: Library of Congress, Cataloging Distribution Service, 1999.

Olson, Nancy B., ed. *Cataloging Internet Resources: A Manual and Practical Guide.* 2nd ed. Dublin, Ohio: OCLC, 1997. See: http://www.oclc.org/oclc/man/9256cat/toc.htm

Use of Fixed Fields 006/007/008 and Leader Codes in CONSER Records. See: http://lcweb.loc.gov/acq/conser/ffuse.html

Weitz, Jay. *Cataloging Electronic Resources: OCLC-MARC Coding Guidelines.* Revised October 25, 1999. See: http://www.oclc.org/oclc/cataloging/type.htm

---

APPENDIX 2
Two Approaches to Bibliographic Description

OCLC: 15088415   Rec stat: c
Entered: 19870120   Replaced: 20000214   Used: 20000208
Type: a   ELvl: Srce: d   GPub: Ctrl: Lang: eng
BLvl: s   Form: Conf: 0   Freq: s   MRec: Ctry: enk
S/L: 0   Orig: EntW: Regl: x   ISSN: z   Alph: a
Desc: a   SrTp: p Cont: DtSt: c   Dates: 1987,9999

```
 1 010     89-655551 $z sn87-21196
 2 040     EUN $c EUN $d MDU $d IUL $d HUL $d NLM $d NYG $d AGL
$d NSD $d NST $d NSD $d NST $d COO $d NST $d DLC $d NST $d DLC $d
NST $d NLM $d DLC $d IUL $d WAU $d TJC $d WAU $d OCL  $d MYG $d
UMC
 3 007     c $b r $d c $e n        [007 for the remote version]
 4 007     c $b o $d u $e g $f u   [007 for accompanying CD-ROMs; see line 28]
 5 012     4 $i 8708 $k 1 $m 1
 6 022     0950-1991
 7 030     DEVPED
 8 032     279800 $b USPS
 9 042     lc $a nsdp
10 050 00  QL951 $b .D38
11 060 00  W1 $b DE997NR
12 069 0   8701744
13 069 1   SR0058569
14 070 0   QL951.D38
15 072  0  X300
16 082 00  611.013
17 090     $b
```

EXAMPLE 1   Single Record Approach: Noting Existence of Electronic Version on the Bibliographic Record for the Print Version

18 049   MUUA
19 130 0   Development (Cambridge, England)
20 210 0   Development $b (Camb.)
21 222 0   Development $b (Cambridge)
22 245 00   Development.
23 260   [Cambridge, Cambridgeshire] : $b Company of Biologists, $c c1987-
24 300   v. : $b ill. ; $c 28 cm.
25 310   24 no. a year, $b 1997-
26 321   Twelve no. a year, $b 1987-1996
27 362 0   Vol. 99 (1) (Jan. 1987)-
28 500   Some issues accompanied by CD-ROM.
29 500   Title from cover.
30 510 1   Excerpta medica $b 1987-
31 510 2   Biological abstracts $x 0006-3169 $b 1987-
32 510 2   Chemical abstracts $x 0009-2258 $b 1987-
33 510 2   Life sciences collection $b 1987-
34 515   Vol. 123 complete in one issue.
35 525   Supplements accompany some vols., <1987>-1989.
36 530   Also available on the World Wide Web to subscribers; articles in PDF
format.
37 555 8   Subject and author index: Integrated annual indexes, subjects and
authors, or journals published by the Company of Biologists, <1998->
38 580   Vols. for 1990-   have separately published supplement with title:
Development (Cambridge, England). Supplement.
39 650 0   Developmental biology $x Periodicals.
40 650 0   Embryology $x Periodicals.
41 650 0   Morphology (Animals) $x Periodicals.
42 650 2   Biology $x periodicals.
43 650 2   Growth $x periodicals.
44 710 2   Company of Biologists.
45 770 1 $t Development (Cambridge, England). Supplement $w (DLC)sn
91033536 $w (OCoLC)24559381
46 776 1 $t Development (Cambridge, England : Online) $w (DLC)sn
96047027
47 780 00 $t Journal of embryology and experimental morphology $x 0022-
0752 $w (DLC) 56045668 $w (OCoLC)1696115
48 787 1 $t Integrated annual indexes, subject and authors, of journals
published by the Company of Biologists Limited $x 1466-6146 $w (DLC)sn
99050040
49 850   AAP $a AU $a Aru $a ArU-M ...
50 856 41 $u http://www.biologists.com/Development/

```
OCLC: 34506804      Rec stat:  c
Entered:  19960403    Replaced:  19991129    Used:  20000128
Type: a   ELvl:   Srce: d  GPub:    Ctrl:    Lang: eng
BLvl: s   Form:    Conf: 0  Freq: s  MRec:   Ctry: enk
S/L:  0   Orig:    EntW:    Regl: r  ISSN:   Alph:
Desc: a   SrTp: p  Cont:    DtSt: c  Dates: 19uu,9999
 1 010     sn96-47027
 2 040     WAU $c WAU $d OCL  $d IUL
 3 006     [m     c     ]
 4 007     c $b r $d c $e n
 5 022     $y 0950-1991
 6 042     lcd
 7 050 14  QL951 $b .D385
 8 060     W1 $b DE997NR
 9 090     $b
10 049     MUUA
11 130 0   Development (Cambridge, England : Online)
12 245 00  Development $h [computer file].
13 260     Cambridge, U.K. : $b Company of Biologists,
14 310     Semimonthly, $b 1997-
15 321     Monthly, $b <1993>-1996
16 362 1   Electronic coverage as of Nov. 8, 1999: vol. 115, no. 1 (1992)-
17 500     Description based on: Vol. 117, 1 (1993); title from issue contents
page.
18 515     Issues for  -1993 issued in 3 v. per year.
19 516 8   Electronic journal (.pdf, .html files)
20 520     Contains article full-text and abstracts of older issues; abstracts of
current and prepublication issues. Includes WAIS-searching of subject and author
indexes.
21 530     Online version of: Development (Cambridge, England).
22 538     Mode of access: World Wide Web.
23 538     System requirements: Adobe Acrobat to view full-text of articles in
pdf file format.
24 650 0   Developmental biology $v Periodicals.
25 650 0   Embryology $v Periodicals.
26 650 0   Morphology (Animals) $v Periodicals.
27 650 2   Biology $x electronic journals.
28 650 2   Growth $x electronic journals.
29 710 2   Company of Biologists.
30 776 1   $t Development (Cambridge, England) $w (DLC)   89655551
$w(OCoLC)15088415
31 856 40  $u http://www.biologists.com/Development/
32 856 40  $u http://www.cob.org.uk/Development/
33 936     Vol. 126, 22 (1999) LIC
```

EXAMPLE 2   Separate Record Approach: Record for the Online Version

10

Nuts and Bolts

Public Service in an Electronic Environment

RAYE LYNN THOMAS

WHY ACQUIRE AND CATALOG ELECTRONIC SERIALS?

We are moving rapidly away from an information environment in which e-journals are an experimental or backup format to an environment in which e-journals are the primary choice. Whenever possible, we should offer our users the added value inherent in the electronic format—the power to link in-text citations to a reference list, or the capability to magnify or rotate graphic illustrations within an article, or the ability to move easily from one article to another and to relevant Web sites. The viewpoint presented here does not mean to ignore the complex issues of pricing, archiving, reliable connectivity, and licensing of e-journals. These are indeed serious issues and in need of much attention at the professional level within both publishing and librarianship. From the users' viewpoint, however, the technology is highly desirable, and as professionals we should make every effort to overcome the obstacles.

In considering the pros and cons of acquiring electronic journals, we can focus on the idea of students as consumers of higher education and make valid points regarding the need to remain current and competitive with other institutions. We can also discuss the phenomenon of competition among libraries, bookstores, and commercial Internet sites

Based on a presentation made at the Third Electronic Serials Institute, "Blazing the Trail: Electronic Serials from Acquisition to Access," April 16–17, 1999, Portland, Oregon.

in the provision of information. Or we can emphasize the service aspect of an academic library, which includes state-of-the-art technology.

Libraries are also being pushed toward e-journals by curricular demands at their institutions. Faculty are encouraged to design courses to capitalize on technology. Increasingly, public services librarians must instruct students in locating and printing course syllabi and assignments that are obtainable primarily from class Web pages. Assignments in which students must locate a full-text electronic article and post it to the class discussion group, and similar Web-based research assignments, are becoming common. The library at Sonoma State University began providing access to full-text periodicals and other material through Lexis/Nexis in 1986; faculty quickly incorporated use of this database into their course work, sometimes framing research assignments around it. Although formal statistics are not available, subjective impressions of the reference staff are that users prefer full-text resources whenever possible.

Student Expectations

Librarians have been on the continuum of change that is occurring in publishing, but many students have not. This is especially true of younger students who have come of age in the online culture and may have come from schools that relied upon Internet resources in the absence of substantial print collections. This expectation is played out repeatedly in library instruction rooms and reference areas filled with undergraduates, who are frequently surprised and dismayed to discover they cannot simply click on a hyperlink to access full-text after locating the bibliographic information. We've also done our part to heighten user expectations by providing electronic and remote access to reference resources and periodical indexes. By offering Web-based indexes but not full-text, we may be guilty of sending mixed messages and confusing students who expect to complete their research process in front of a computer. With all sorts of full-text information available on the Internet, many students assume they will be able to obtain scholarly research articles. Additionally, they know that high-resolution graphics, sound, and video are commonly found elsewhere with their Web browsers. So why not in the library? To an undergraduate with a paper due in two days, a lengthy explanation of licensing and archiving issues falls on deaf ears.

All students may not walk into the library with such expectations, but all are thrilled by the discovery that full-text is a click away from their search results, and, furthermore, that they can e-mail these articles to themselves. This can be a useful "hook" in a library instruction session, especially for students who believe that library research will be hopelessly boring or confusing. The availability of electronic full-text that can be downloaded or e-mailed never fails to impress and reliably engages the students' interest in library research. For a typical undergraduate just learning research methods, the library can be intimidating. We should do our best to take advantage of existing tools that make research as easy as possible, so that students can focus instead on mastering search strategies and learning to evaluate content.

Distance Education

Many academic institutions now offer distance education courses, and with this comes the obligation to provide library resources. Typically, these courses are designed for working professionals or remote populations and rely primarily on asynchronous class discussions, video conferencing, and e-mail interaction with faculty and reference librarians. Students are encouraged to locate a nearby host library; for some services, such as interlibrary loan book pickup, this works well. Many distance learners, however, are hard-pressed to find time to travel regularly to a host library with an adequate journal collection. Although turnaround time for document delivery or interlibrary loan is continually shrinking, it still imposes a constraint on these students and also precludes their ability to assess the usefulness of a particular research article immediately. In reference interchanges with distance education faculty and students, a constant question is: "Where's the full text?" One way to provide library service equivalent to that provided to on-campus students is to offer remote access to electronic journals. Remote access to full-text can provide the following benefits:

Lower child-care expenses: This may seem trivial, but many students juggle jobs and parenting along with their course load, and remote access to full-text really serves this population.

Freedom from library hours: The announcement that the library is closing often produces a bit of panic in the reference area. Last-minute researchers are grateful to learn about the full-text databases that are accessible from remote locations.

Scholarly articles on demand: Along with the equity issue, distance education students are often reluctant to pursue a research question beyond what is immediately available. In addition, educating students regarding intellectual property is an ongoing issue, whether in the print or digital format. While the temptation to plagiarize may be greater in an electronic full-text environment, a valid counter-argument may be made about the benefit of electronic full-text when references are cited accurately. Remote full-text allows off-campus researchers to use authoritative and appropriate resources.

USER AUTHENTICATION

IP Authentication, Passwords, and Proxies

Most vendors now offer a variety of authentication methods that allow libraries to work within their particular system capabilities. Many institutions have the capability to authenticate at the campus account level through kerberos, a network authentication protocol; others must rely on vendor-issued passwords or IP authentication.[1] Although IP authentication involves maintenance issues, using a proxy server to authenticate remote users and to prevent incidental use of some databases appears to be the most practical access solution. The proxy server screens users by domain name and requires use of one user name and password for all databases. As new databases are added, their domain names must be added to the proxy script. Most often this does not prove too burdensome a task, but it might be a compelling reason to work with aggregators rather than individual publishers. Electronic products not accessible via an IP authentication process require passwords for access.

Managing passwords as they change each semester is time-consuming. Users must be alerted to the changes, for example, on the library's home page or in library instruction sessions. Campus IDs must be checked for currency, and an instruction sheet for proxy setup distributed. In the interest of minimizing bureaucracy, password distribution should be handled in the same area in which all students must confirm library privileges. Users must activate the proxy within their browser preferences; for some, this requires instruction, although most users have adapted to this process fairly easily. This instructional need also allows contact between reference staff and a portion of the student body not often otherwise seen. Connectivity questions often bring students to the library when research questions don't. A basic instructional handout as well as a more detailed one on troubleshooting, solutions for common connectivity problems, and error messages should be made available at the reference desk and posted on the Web.

Licensing Considerations

There are a vast number of possible licensing arrangements, and it is very important, from the public service perspective, to understand certain contract specifics. One pricing model relates to IP authentication and concerns the designated range of IP addresses determined by the class of the license. A class B license is more extensive, truncating after the network identifier or second set of numbers in the IP addressing system, whereas a class C license is more specific, truncating after the third set of numbers, identifying a particular portion of the network, and encompassing a smaller set of workstations. Although it may be economically tempting to purchase a class C license, the more restrictive license can create confusion. For example, a class C license for a specialized chemistry journal may make sense economically, but will confound chemistry students if they try to access the journal from a location outside the IP range. Administering such restrictions obviously adds another variable to an already complex process. It is important to designate one person in the library to maintain a list of the library's needs to be negotiated with each contract. This point person should work closely with public services, so that those on the front line are aware of any unusual contract restrictions and can assure that none are impractical to enforce.

Selective Access

Most vendors are respectful of the impracticality of monitoring incidental in-house use in a library where the workstations aren't enclosed. This is one of the essentials of a contract for online journals. Not only is such use difficult to enforce, but especially in the case of e-journals, it could have a negative effect on community borrowers. It is important to consider fully the ramifications of selective access. If there are contractual restrictions on incidental use, or if the library has other reasons for restricting access to certain resources, it is possible to set up selective access through a proxy server script. In programmer's terms, this is known as conditional logic. For example, if the IP address is [remote], then send login through the proxy server. However, if the IP address is [local], but the domain name is [www.specificvendor.com], then also send login through the proxy server. In addition to honoring contractual restrictions, this mechanism may be used to limit use of pay-per-view databases and those with limited simultaneous logins, thus ensuring priority for primary clientele. In addition to the Web page that centralizes access to a library's subscription databases, a separate page may be created listing publicly accessible databases not requiring a password. Databases may be grouped topically, and those databases that are freely available, such as PubMed and the public versions of ERIC and CARL UnCover, are so indicated. Consequently, community users and public services staff don't have to remember the access specifics of each database.

HARDWARE

Workstations

Meeting demand for workstations in a library with a large number of databases and other Web resources can be a struggle. Although a campus environment may have several computer labs, they are frequently in use for classes or instructional software applications. It also seems that many students prefer to work in the library, where they have access to reference and technical assistance. To satisfy hardware needs on a limited budget, networked computers may be used to replace obsolete terminals. Not only are they less expensive to purchase than PCs, networked computers are also efficient in terms of maintenance. Software resides on a central server, so if users change preferences or otherwise disrupt the system, only a workstation reboot is required to restore original settings. If no floppy drives are purchased, there is no downloading capability, but this should not prove to be a significant drawback, because users can print or e-mail from all databases. Unexpected difficulties, such as the inability to print from selective databases or the inability to type in a dialog box without first activating the cursor by clicking on the desktop, may occur but should be fairly easy to resolve. Another method for maximizing hardware inventory may be to convert previously dedicated CD-ROM network stations to multipurpose workstations, because these are now underutilized with the migration of many bibliographic databases to the Web.

Screen resolution is an important consideration for displaying illustrations from online journals, and students must often be reassured when working on older workstations that the printed version of a graphic will be of higher quality than the version being viewed onscreen. That, of course, assumes users will print out articles with graphics. Before relying completely on an online version of a journal, it is essential to know that workstation monitors will display charts, graphs, and photos adequately. When working with a new vendor or publisher, librarians should request a trial subscription to determine whether the graphics display is of sufficient quality.

Adequate Server Capacity

Public services librarians should know the capabilities and limitations of a system as well as understand the technical implications of collection development decisions. Online journal access will increase server demand. The server at Sonoma State currently allows 32,000 simultaneous connections, which frequently translates into 8,000 simultaneous users because many transactions involve up to four connections. The system administrator has noticed slowness when there are between 2,000 and 4,000 simultaneous users, and users notice a degradation in response time when there are more than 4,000. To support those 8,000 users fully, a server with a gigabyte of memory is recommended. To plan reliable connectivity and reasonable response time for an online journal collection requires factoring the transaction demand on the server from all resources along with the count of the total user population.

Systematic Replacement

It is wise to develop guidelines for systematic replacement of equipment or to establish a refresh rate. The main question to ask is: "How old is the oldest computer you care to or are able to support in your library?" If the answer is five years, for example, one fifth of the library's systems budget should be set aside annually for equipment replacement. As those who reboot aging computers know, a five-year refresh rate is fairly modest.

Staffing

It may seem odd to consider staffing in a discussion of hardware, but it is very pertinent, because staffing relates directly to the quantity of hardware that can be supported. Providing adequate staff to assist with reference and technical questions over a large physical spread of workstations is an issue to consider. Determining a realistic ratio of workstations to staff, in terms of reference services, technical assistance, and systems maintenance, is very important. Reference and technical support, both for on-site and remote users, is an additional factor to consider in the move to online journals.

SOFTWARE

Uniformity of software is one of the greatest challenges facing public services librarians, and it relates directly to the hardware refresh rate. The need to purchase or replace workstations on some sort of revolving schedule means that library staff must be familiar with a variety of platforms, some of which cannot support the latest version of a particular browser or operating system. In a library instructional lab in which students work along with the instructor, the need to support multiple versions is even more critical. Although some of the differences in look and feel may seem trivial, such as those in printing dialog boxes or in the location of some menu items, they may be enough to confuse novice users. Librarians should strive to maintain as much uniformity at the desktop as possible, even if it means delaying the installation of the latest version of a browser application.

Security software is used to prevent access to mail preferences and the hard drive on public workstations. Security settings allow students to download files to a designated folder on the desktop or to a floppy. Access to printer preferences is allowed, because there are so many variables in making a legible print, especially of a Web page orientation, gray scale, or size. At Sonoma State, librarians had to discontinue using security software on the PCs because of incompatibilities with various applications, which caused the workstations to freeze frequently. The major sacrifice was the ease of restoring preferences and applications if these were altered; the problem was resolved by designing a system rebuild that restores applications and preferences from a floppy disk and that takes only fifteen minutes to accomplish.

Many security software applications provide an administrative module for centrally upgrading applications and changing preferences. This is particularly useful in areas with large numbers of workstations, where making changes would otherwise represent a significant workload for systems staff. As noted earlier, one advantage of choosing networked computers is that as thin client technology, they operate from a central server and require only a reboot to reinstate their original settings, thus significantly reducing administrative workload.

USER INTERFACE: SEARCH ENGINES

In a 1997 article, John H. Barnes commented that "aggregation of electronic journals into a common format with a consistent interface is key to making them efficiently usable by the researcher and cost-effective for the library."[2] This is critical in minimizing frustration both for the user community and for public services staff, and is a compelling reason to work with aggregators or consider a Z39.50 interface. Clearly, some users are sophisticated regarding phrase searching, Boolean operators, truncation, and wild card symbols, but most aren't. Librarians should make every effort to persuade vendors to standardize or at least provide multiple options for command syntax, to account for the most common variants. Pull-down menu choices for search operators are a definite improvement over proliferation of nonstandardized command-based systems, which require first a hunt for online help and then a search through an index to locate proper syntax and symbols. Truncation and wild card options should also be made more apparent, not only for ease of use by students, but also for the sanity of public services staff.

Even more critical for novice users is the need for predictability of methods for marking records for display, downloading, and e-mailing.

Fortunately, these features have become relatively standardized. Internal e-mail features are also an improvement, and usually clearer for students to understand than the browser commands and on-screen instructions. Of course, some libraries currently resolve nonstandardization with a Z39.50 interface. California State University is about to launch a union catalog that will provide access to full-text collections through a Z39.50 interface. In some cases, the option to use the native interface of these databases will also remain, and it will be interesting to note user preferences on these.

Although simplification and standardization in the provision of e-journals are usually preferred, when considering file formats, a variety of options seems a better accommodation based on the variety of content, the differing needs of researchers, and the range of their technical skills. Ideally, ASCII, page image, and SGML should all be options, clearly identified, with ASCII as the default option. Compromise on that ideal is usually necessary, but it is imperative that omissions of images within a plain text article are clearly noted, and that a page image format can be viewed with a standard PDF viewer. E-mailing PDF documents is frequently problematic, however, so SGML may ultimately be the best solution for e-mailing articles with graphics. Certainly, the inclusion of easily retrievable, high-quality graphics is key to a successful transition from print to electronic articles.

Standard helper applications, viewers, and plug-ins are also important to acceptance of electronic journals by many users. A good choice for a PDF viewer is a standard, nonproprietary application with which users are likely to be familiar in other settings. If a journal requires other plug-ins for full use, librarians should look at the capabilities of lower-end workstations in public areas and make decisions accordingly. If a proprietary viewer or printing system is required for a publication, think carefully before purchase. Lack of standardization creates a potentially onerous maintenance workload as well as a significant user support issue. Even with security software, applications occasionally disappear, are moved from their proper place, or become corrupted. Staff must not only keep these applications functioning and current for in-house users, but must also be able to explain installation and use to remote users.

BIBLIOGRAPHIC ACCESS

Cataloging electronic serials requires policy decisions as well as technical ones, and catalogers and public services staff need an ongoing dialog regarding complex bibliographic access issues. Should freely available e-journals be cataloged, or should cataloging be limited only to those titles received on library subscriptions? Should a separate full-text database be implemented as well as links within bibliographic records to identify full-text in collections? If so, where within the library Web pages should this be located? Should URLs for journals within collections point to the initial page for the database? Should links from indexing and abstracting services be provided? The questions seem endless, and decisions are best made with pooled cataloging and public services expertise as well as the expertise of the library's Webmaster.

OPAC display is another area in which pooled expertise is very effective. Working sessions in which the cataloger brings various examples of note fields and entries for multiple formats to reference staff meetings make it possible for staff to examine the options together. This promotes sound decision making and also serves as a great educational opportunity for public services staff, who become much more effective at locating and interpreting bibliographic records for the public.

BIBLIOGRAPHIC MAINTENANCE

Some bibliographic maintenance issues can be resolved at the onset by contractual specifications. An important one is to require PURLs, or stable and durable URLs. Although some adequate link-checking applications exist, staff time is still required to review results and make changes in what could easily be an overwhelming workload. It is far better to obtain a vendor's commitment to maintaining stability.

An ongoing issue from the public services perspective is content disparities between print and electronic versions of a title. It is helpful to indicate selective coverage of a title, if known, but journal lists provided by vendors are extensive and thus bound to have some inaccuracies. A fair amount of maintenance is involved in updating content information, but doing so means that users will have more confidence in the accuracy of the information. Additionally, within collections, content is sometimes added or deleted without notification, and it is not always possible for a vendor to provide advance notification of such changes, because this is a decision of individual publishers. However, it is not unreasonable to request advance notification when possible and at least timely notification upon occurrence. It is also reasonable to expect vendors to provide accurate descriptions of electronic content, such as whether advertisements, letters to the editor, or news briefs are included.

Whether journals are hosted on a centralized server or on distributed servers can have significant maintenance implications for public services staff and should be taken into account when making subscription decisions. We've all experienced disruptions in service when a publisher's server is down or regularized downtime while new data are uploaded. A centralized server that has proven reliable and robust, with a 24/7 service guarantee, has become more common and thus is a realistic expectation. If the journal collection will be hosted on numerous servers, problems are compounded in terms of monitoring outages and user notification of same as well as the obvious implications for instruction. At Sonoma State, reference staff scheduled for the first hour each day routinely check connections, but as host servers proliferate, it becomes more difficult to be thorough. As a result, staff members rely on user reports of connectivity difficulties, which are then followed up by contacting vendor customer support. Responsibility for such reports is best assigned to one person, or a small group of people, to avoid redundant efforts and to provide some continuity in interactions with vendor technical support. A Web-based form containing customer support contacts for all vendors, hours of their availability, and identifying account numbers is handy not only for the primary contact person, but also for evening and weekend staff who may have only an occasional, but immediate, need to deal with a connectivity problem. Access to account information can be passworded at the local level to prevent unauthorized use. Many vendors also provide electronic discussion lists for customers through which planned outages are announced, and it is useful to have a designated participant in these services who forwards necessary information to all public services staff.

PRINTING, DOWNLOADING, AND E-MAILING RESULTS

Thus far, there is no indication that the advent of e-journals has inspired another leap toward a paperless society, although the ability to e-mail full-text has provided some relief for libraries in which printing solutions are frequently imperfect. Workstations with dedicated printers mean maintenance and instructional issues for public services staff. On the other hand, centralized printing requires an effective way to clearly identify print jobs. When network traffic is high, print commands can queue up and stall, and staff must manually clear print jobs from individual workstations. In short, unless the library can afford to purchase a high-tech printing solution, significant maintenance issues will probably be inherent in any method, so decisions may best depend on other factors. One factor critical for e-journals is quality. A 600–1200 dpi printer is necessary to ensure high-quality graphics, and if the library cannot afford to purchase a fleet of these, it might be best to consider networked printing or a print station. The major problem with a print station, or a select group of workstations with printers, is that people must know in advance that they want to print, otherwise they become frustrated when they have to recreate their search on another workstation in order to print the results. The ideal is a standardized work area with print capability at all workstations.

The popularity of downloading articles and bibliographic records has clearly diminished, now that people have the ability to e-mail results by using either the e-mail function provided within subscription databases or the "send page" function of the Web browser. The internal e-mail function is generally recommended because it is usually a simpler process, but if patrons do use the browser e-mail function, they should also quote the attachment within the body of the message. This provides reassurance that the document will truly arrive, because it is visible to the patron. It also relieves a novice user of the anxiety of working with e-mail attachments. In the interests of preventing misuse and protecting user privacy, e-mail settings within the Web browser are locked by the security software. Before these restrictions were in place, patrons would frequently forget to remove their personal information from the mail preferences. Settings are now configured generically, indicating "Public User" as the sender, and a reply to these messages will generate a return message to the effect that the reply is not reaching the sender.

The capacity of campus e-mail accounts, most of which are quite small, has become less of a problem as students rely more on commercial ISPs rather than campus accounts. In the past, if students attempted to mail themselves a lengthy file, it would simply not arrive in their account, and there was no indication of an error at the time the document was sent. This is also something to be investigated before a library relies on an e-journal collection.

At Sonoma State University, a classified staff position of Information Technology Consultant provides high-level technical assistance and instruction within the reference department. This staff member is responsible for developing and maintaining platform-specific instructional guides for downloading, e-mailing, and printing. These guides are posted at each workstation along with a guide for opening e-mail attachments. All guides are available as handouts at the reference desk and are posted on the library's Web pages for remote availability. As browsers or operating systems are upgraded, it is essential to revise these and make sure that details are correct. Subtle variations may seem insignificant, but can be quite confusing to a novice user who attempts to move through the steps literally.

TECHNICAL SUPPORT FOR USERS

It is important to determine and define the capabilities of the staff, whether they are universal or selective, and make them known to the users. It is probably more realistic, from a public services perspective, to provide quality support for a discrete set of applications than attempt to support everything available in the universe of browsers and helper applications. The nature of reference service has shifted considerably over the past few years, with reference staff spending increasing amounts of time assisting patrons with the technical side of their research. Not only do public services staff field myriad technical support questions in the reference area, they are also expected to assist remote users by telephone and e-mail. To provide effective technical support to the growing population of remote users, staff members must be able to reconstruct particular problems and situations, and this requires access to the same set of applications available to the remote user. Unless the library is able to dedicate a workstation and a knowledgeable systems person to remote support for a broad range of software and hardware, it is probably better to define capabilities based on applications used in-house. The proprietary browsers of some Internet service providers are particularly problematic, because they also require a subscription. At Sonoma State, librarians attempted, unsuccessfully, to secure complimentary access in order to troubleshoot, because without the ability to reconstruct a problem firsthand, the likelihood of resolving it is slim. A pattern of incompatibilities emerged between some proprietary browsers and the library's subscription databases, so ultimately it seemed better to recommend a generic browser, even though some users may be reluctant to change. It is important, though, to monitor the application preferences of the user population and reconsider the repertoire when demand reaches critical mass. For example, the entire campus clearly supported Netscape as the browser of choice, but so many are now using Internet Explorer that librarians felt compelled to support this application as well.

Staff Training

In addition to content and interface knowledge, a basic level of technical proficiency that includes, at a minimum, downloading, printing, and e-mailing is necessary for all public services staff. To minimize the anxiety that arises with this complexity, it is useful to provide time for staff members to learn a new system before it is made publicly available. Regular in-service training, including refreshers, is helpful, especially because interface upgrades seem to be occurring with increasing frequency. Librarians should also take advantage of in-depth professional training that may be offered by a vendor. Beyond establishing a basic level of proficiency through training, having designated content specialists helps make all public services staff comfortable with the fast-moving technology. Establishing an on-call support group to assist with difficult or time-consuming technical questions as they arise is also a good idea. Of course, remote access demands increased technical support for remote users, and this has largely become a routine telephone transaction, incorporated into regular reference service. As with in-person assistance, advanced or complicated questions are referred to the second-level technical support group.

TECHNICAL SUPPORT FOR STAFF

Whatever the organizational structure of the library, a close relationship between systems and public services staff is needed for smooth operations. It is essential to plan cooperatively for system and hardware upgrades, so that no one is taken by surprise. Systems personnel can also be a resource for public services staff training, especially when system changes are made.

Division of technical support responsibilities between the library and the campus information technology department may be difficult to maintain, as e-mail and software applications become increasingly intertwined with library research and the idea of a scholar's workstation is realized. This certainly supports the decision many campuses have made to merge the two areas and establish an information commons. Barring this kind of organizational restructuring, a close relationship between units or departments is still critical. E-journals make the library even more dependent on campus infrastructure, and up-to-date information is essential for effective library operations and planning. Advance notification of local system outages, changes in infrastructure that affect library connectivity, or additions or changes in campus IP addresses are just a few reasons why ongoing communication is important.

Consideration of technical support offered by vendors should be an intrinsic part of the decision-making process in collection development and accounted for in contractual agreements. Some questions that particularly affect the public services staff are:

What are the hours of technical support by telephone for our time zone? Do these coincide with hours of heavy demand in the library?

Is there a guaranteed turnaround time for e-mail technical support?

What provision is made for notification of interface changes, especially those that would require local hardware or software upgrades?

Is a trainer available to come to the library and train staff, especially when a new interface is involved?

CONCLUSION

In an article on full-text databases, Carol Tenopir mentioned a survey in which many public and academic librarians stated that electronic full-text was the primary preference of their patrons.[3] In an ideal world, libraries would be able to purchase both print and electronic versions of all resources. Unfortunately, that is not possible for many libraries. Libraries with static budgets cannot usually support redundancy and must make some difficult choices between print and electronic access. Students and faculty make it clear on a daily basis that there is no turning back from electronic journals. Such demand provides great impetus for working toward resolution of obstacles to this exciting transition, and librarians are undoubtedly capable of doing so.

NOTES

1. For a detailed explanation see: http://www.nrl.navy.mil/CCS/people/kenh/ kerberos-faq.html or the kerberos website at: http://web.mit.edu/kerberos/www/

2. John H. Barnes, "One Giant Leap, One Small Step: Continuing the Migration to Electronic Journals," *Library Trends* 45, no. 3 (winter 1997): 412.

3. Carol Tenopir, "Online Databases: Should We Cancel Print?" *Library Journal* 124, no. 14 (September 1, 1999): 138–139.

11

Another New Frontier
Trailblazing Electronically

THOMAS W. LEONHARDT

Electronic journals have been around at least since the early 1990s, and probably as early as the late 1980s, beginning as ASCII text files sent to subscribers via e-mail as part of an electronic discussion list.[1] Early users of the Internet, with time, access, and imagination, saw electronic journals as the wave of the future. The hyperbole surrounding the Internet suggested that the future was now, and that if librarians did not immediately and unequivocally jump onto the moving train of change, they would be left at the station, never mind that the train had no posted destination. Experience suggests that few changes are so precipitous and clear in their implications as to allow no waiting. There will be another train, and its ride may be smoother and with a clearer destination.

We have learned much since electronic serials became a reality, but the more we learn and the farther we go, the less certain we are of our destination. Technology is indeed moving at a terrific pace and threatens to grant us our wishes. History is about choices made and consequences that followed. Our job is to be wary of the possible consequences, not to assume that they will all be good, and to plan in ways that improve our lot and not simply abandon the past because it is behind us.

Based on a presentation made at the Third Electronic Serials Institute, "Blazing the Trail: Electronic Serials from Acquisition to Access," April 16–17, 1999, Portland, Oregon.

158

BACKGROUND

In the early 1990s, a report from the MIT Electronic Journals Task Force stated that "there are only about 30 titles in existence and only six of these are refereed."[2] Included were journals in electronic form only as well as those in both electronic form and either paper or fiche formats. Quoting Ann Okerson, the task force noted that the "greatest contributions [of electronic journals] are not that they have solved many of the problems of the current publishing system—or of the networked world—but that they are brave, exciting, innovative experiments which give us hope of doing so."[3]

In that same report, the task force noted that it shared some of the concerns of Charles Bailey, editor of the *Public-Access Computer Systems Review,* also published electronically as PACS-L, one of the earliest and most popular of electronic serials, who wrote:

> As librarians we must decide what role we are to play in the network information environment. Will we take an active role as trailblazer and trail guide, assisting users in identifying and accessing remote electronic serials and other network resources? . . . Will we help shape the future of electronic serials?[4]

Okerson and Bailey were both very involved with electronic serials from the beginning and recognized their importance. Both noted that such a format did not solve the existing problems, but that librarians needed to be actively involved with this new format in the best interests of library users. Librarians took up the challenge and have contributed greatly to the development of this new medium and to its bibliographic control.

DEALING WITH THE UNKNOWN

Electronic serials, rather than solving problems associated with serials in general, such as availability, cost, or their role in tenure decisions, have added to those problems and made them more complex. So, despite roughly a decade of experience with electronic serials, it still seems accurate and appropriate to portray work with them as trailblazing, exploring, leading the way. In fact, although it was the third such institute, the 1999 ALCTS Electronic Serials Institute, held in Portland, Oregon, was titled, "Blazing the Trail: Electronic Serials from Acquisition to Access," and not solely as an allusion to the Lewis and Clark expedition that enduringly linked Oregon and the pioneer spirit. How many more electronic serials institutes will ALCTS sponsor before the territory is settled? The end of the novelty of it all may be in sight, but serials work is never done. Perhaps electronic issues will settle into ALA, the North American Serials Interest Group (NASIG), and other niches so that isolated institutes will no longer be needed, but that day has not yet come.

Blazing a trail connotes the exploration of new territory, the territory ahead. It suggests leading the way, taking risks, striking out for the unknown in search of opportunity, a fresh start—perhaps fame and fortune. This analogy seems a more useful way to consider what is going on in the management of electronic serials than merely talking about change.

Why is the trailblazing metaphor preferable to ones about being left in a train station? First of all, it is a more realistic way of looking at how librarians have traditionally dealt with change. There have been the leaders and early adopters; there have been their supporters, waiting for the right moment to follow; and there have been the skeptics, raising critical points and concerns that, rather than slowing progress, have provided tools that the leaders could use to their advantage. Everyone need not be a trailblazer or even immediately follow the leader, just because someone is out there alone and reporting gold, fertile soil, acres of clams, and other treasures.

Trailblazing is a positive, adventurous approach to the unknown, but it is understood that pioneers possess, in addition to courage and perseverance, pathfinding skills, experience, and tools that they know how to use. There are ways to deal with the unknown. We use foresight, knowledge, intelligence, skill, determination, and courage. Trailblazers are, in a word, leaders and are not content to simply react to change and the unknown out of fear or intimidation. In this relatively uncharted electronic serials wilderness, how do we blaze the trail? We really began to acquire the necessary tools and experience decades ago. We began to prepare for electronic serials with the introduction of the MARC record; ISBD; the ISSN; AACR2 and all its subsequent revisions and interpretations; the serials modules that we now find in integrated, automated library systems; and in our experience acquiring and cataloging reprinted material, microforms, audiovisual materials, and realia. Librarians have been trailblazers and pathfinders from the very beginning of the electronic age, and the work done from librarianship's earliest days has provided the knowledge and expertise that we bring to bear on electronic serials. We have blazed the trail by applying each new technological advance to particular problems. Often, the problems revolve around labor-intensive operations that can be improved through automation. But in other instances, while solving one problem, we create others and must look to our own experience to solve them. In other words, applying technology to a manual procedure may introduce complexities that must, in turn, be handled according to basic tenets of practice and principles of service.

Acquisitions

Part of our explorations today that are producing some unexpected results have to do with serials prices. Until 1972, the average price of a U.S. hardbound book was slightly more than the average price of a U.S. periodical. In 1971, the average periodical cost $11.66, and the average hardcover book cost $13.25. In 1972, the periodical price jumped to $13.23, and the book price *dropped* to $12.99.[5] From then on, periodical prices increased steeply and relentlessly, without any relief, until, finally, librarians took notice.

The first response was to throw money at the problem—in hindsight, our first mistake. We then began cancellation programs (which continue to this day) that were coupled with additional funds, and we ended up spending more and buying less. Then, like members of the UN or NATO trying to stop a civil war, we tried diplomacy, but to no avail. The responses offered to pleas for some kind of relief were that no relief was possible—that increases were driven by the cost of paper one year, ink the next, editorial services after that, the decreasing value of the dollar for several years, and so on until it became a given that the average price of periodicals, especially in certain fields, would go up by 10 percent or so a year as a matter of course with no justification being given or even expected.

With the advent of desktop publishing and similar opportunities for commercial publishers, it seemed that the computer would solve the pricing and cost dilemma. The thinking was that by using the computer and achieving a certain economy of scale, journals could be produced electronically and cost increases could be brought under control. The publishers' interpretation, however, was that librarians wanted electronic journals and would be willing to pay as much for them as for the print versions, or pay even more for access to both. Pricing and archival concerns aside, publishers' efforts to market electronic periodicals have been favorably received by librarians and library users alike, and some inherent advantages of the electronic over print have been quickly recognized.

Automation has also led to a rejuvenation and proliferation of library consortia as resource-sharing partners. The natural progression led to consortial licensing and purchasing of electronic resources, including periodicals. From our experience in negotiating licensing agreements for individual libraries, we are learning how to write tighter, more advantageous contracts, and learning that united we stand, divided we fall.

Serials acquisition has always been a specialty among librarians. Negotiating, or bidding, for lower service charges is not so very different from negotiating license agreements. There may be more lawyers involved, especially in the early stages, but the principles remain the same. Librarians are blazing a new acquisitions trail using reliable tools and knowledge gained over time. Through eternal vigilance and by sticking together, we have an opportunity to make information affordable again.

Cataloging

If there are parallels to acquiring print and electronic serials, shouldn't we expect similar parallels in cataloging? It seems that the AACR2 definition of a serial is as valid for electronic serials as for any other kind of serial. If an electronic publication does not meet the definition of a serial, it is not a serial and must be handled differently. In fact, serials catalogers are approaching this new format with the kind of expertise and care that we have come to expect of serialists. Librarians learned, in the early days of the Internet, how to cite e-mail, electronic discussion lists, and other electronic documents. They are taking the same approach to electronic serials.

UNITED WE STAND

From thirty electronic serials available in 1992, there are now thousands to choose from. OCLC, as an aggregator, has collected more than a thousand itself. They are Web-based and represent many publishers. The number of electronic journals available on subscription will continue to increase, together with newspapers and popular magazines that are offered free of charge on the Internet. We would be foolish to try to guess where all this will lead. Instead, librarians ought to focus on where we want to go and then lead the way. Rather, librarians should continue to lead the way and not limit our vision to what others tell us is desirable or possible or affordable. Librarians must be vigilant and continue to fight against restrictions of access to information, knowing that when information is priced too high for the library, it is also priced too high for the individual. Information *is* power, and such regulations as the Uniform Computer Information Transactions Act (UCITA) are not designed to allow fair use, but to increase profitability through restrictions on access to information.[6] Knowledge and information are greater foes to tyrants than guns and bullets. There is no surer way to lose freedom than to allow a system that prohibits and inhibits libraries from *freely* dispensing information to all who need it.

As librarians gain experience with electronic serials, we also gain self-confidence and recognize that our many years of experience with library automation, our efforts to work together through consortia, interlibrary loan channels, and continuing education venues, and our commitment to service have prepared us to be trailblazers of the caliber of Lewis and Clark. Librarians are beginning to understand that by working together, we increase our power and, at the same time, our chances of solving our information problems. The pricing spiral cannot continue unabated without creating more harm to library users. Information is for everyone, not just those who can afford it. We are learning, even as the situation changes continuously, that there are limits to what we can and will pay and that consortial licensing, really a form of acquisitions, is providing leverage in library negotiations with publishers. Librarians are learning that, when the price is not right or when the price increase is unreasonable, we must be prepared to say no and walk away. The serials may be virtual but the costs and other issues are real. Given issues such as UCITA, librarians must continue to be trailblazers in the territory of electronic serials in all of their ramifications.

NOTES

1. Ellen Finnie Duranceau, ed., "Third Generation E-journals and Beyond: Is There an Agent in Your Future?" *Electronic Journal Forum* 25, no. 2 (1999): 77.

2. Marlene Manoff and Eileen Dorschner, "Report of the Electronic Journals Task Force MIT Libraries," *Serials Review* 18, no. 1–2 (spring/summer 1992): 114.

3. Ibid., 113.

4. Ibid.

5. *Bowker Annual of Library and Book Trade Information,* 18th ed. (New York: R. R. Bowker, 1973), 330, 332.

6. For an overview of the Uniform Computer Information Transactions Act, see Bryan Carson, "Legally Speaking," *Against the Grain* 11, no. 6 (December 1999–January 2000): 54, 56–58. See also UCITA, Draft for Approval, July 23–30, 1999, at http://www.law.upenn.edu/bll/ulc/ucita/citam99.htm

SOURCES AND RESOURCES

Identifying resources that deal with electronic serials, particularly those available on the Web, is an ambitious undertaking. Part 1 provides annotated references for a few Web-accessible favorites arranged by topic, while part 2 lists more traditional resources.

1: DELVING DEEPER INTO ELECTRONIC SERIALS

The literature on the Web about electronic serials is growing at a prodigious rate, and URLs are notoriously unstable. The following "top picks," all available on the Web, have been selected for their relevance, comprehensiveness, readability, and stability. A thorough consideration of these and other resources may be found in "Electronic Journals: A Selected Resource Guide," available in electronic form and hosted by Harrassowitz Booksellers and Subscription Agents at http://www.harrassowitz. de/ms/ejresguide.html. The guide contains sections on e-journal directories, the history of e-journals, usage studies, standards, legal and business issues, the nature of scholarly publishing, preservation, linking, preprint servers, and discussion lists. The content of the guide is updated periodically, and the links are checked regularly. The following suggestions were extracted from this work.

Part 1 was compiled by Katharina Klemperer and reproduced with the kind permission of Harrassowitz, Booksellers and Subscription Agents. Part 2 was compiled by Pamela Bluh.

Economic Issues

Odlyzko, Andrew M. "The Economics of Electronic Journals." *First Monday* 2, no. 8 (August 4, 1997). This thought-provoking analysis of the current crisis in scholarly publishing has many good references and may be found at http://www.firstmonday.dk/issues/issue2_8/odlyzko/index. html. Reprinted in the *Journal of Electronic Publishing* 4, no. 1 (September 1998); see: http://www.press.umich.edu/jep/04-01/odlyzko.html

Licensing

LIBLICENSE, sponsored by the Council on Library and Information Resources and hosted at Yale University Library, is the place to learn the most about licensing electronic content. This site contains numerous lists of resources and free software to assist in writing a license to electronic content. See: http://www.library.yale.edu/~llicense/index.shtml

Copyright and Rights Management

Gladney, Henry M. "Digital Dilemma: Intellectual Property." *D-Lib Magazine* (December 1999). This is a synopsis and analysis of a report, released in November 1999, prepared by the study committee appointed by the U.S. National Academies to consider the impact of the emerging digital information infrastructure on intellectual property rights. The original report is entitled *The Digital Dilemma: Intellectual Property in the Information Age* and can be found at http://books.nap.edu/html/ digital_dilemma/

Access Control

Lynch, Clifford. "Access Management for Networked Information Resources." *ARL Newsletter,* Issue 201 (December 1998), and *CAUSE/ EFFECT* 21, no. 4 (1998). This is a good primer, moderately technical, on the alternatives for and issues involved in managing access control along with suggestions for solutions. See: http://www.arl.org/newsltr/ 201/cni.html or http://www.educause.edu/ir/library/html/cem9842.html

Cataloging

Olson, Nancy B., ed. *Cataloging Internet Resources: A Manual and Practical Guide,* 2nd ed. Dublin, Ohio: OCLC, 1997. This hands-on guide, containing plenty of examples, was originally developed to aid those participating in the OCLC/U.S. Department of Education–funded project, "Building a Catalog of Internet Resources." It was designed for OCLC users and other project participants, but it has general usefulness. See: http://www.oclc.org/oclc/man/9256cat/toc.htm

Metadata

Cathro, Warwick. "Matching Discovery and Recovery." Paper given at the Standards Australia Seminar, August 1997. This is an excellent introduction to metadata concepts and the Dublin Core initiative. See: http://www.nla.gov.au/nla/staffpaper/cathro3.html

Preservation and Archiving

Bullock, Alison. "Preservation of Digital Information: Issues and Current Status." *Network Notes,* no. 60. Information Technology Services, National Library of Canada. April 22, 1999. Revised May 26, 1999. This review gives, in a nutshell, the major issues involved in preservation of digital content. See: http://www.nlc-bnc.ca/publications/netnotes/notes60.htm

Favorite Discussion Lists

Newsletter on Serials Pricing Issues. Read about it and join at http://www.lib.unc.edu/prices/about.html. Visit the archive at http://www.lib.unc.edu/prices/.

LIBLICENSE-L. Join the list at http://www.library.yale.edu/~llicense/mailing-list.shtml. Visit the archive at http://www.library.yale.edu/~llicense/ListArchives/.

Favorite Online Journal

D-Lib Magazine. "A monthly magazine about innovation and research in digital libraries," based at the Corporation for National Research Initiatives and sponsored by the Defense Advanced Research Projects Agency (DARPA). Nearly every issue contains information relevant to electronic journals. See: http://www.dlib.org

2: TRADITIONAL SOURCES

Alexander, Michael. "Virtual Stacks: Storing and Using Electronic Journals." *Serials* 10, no. 2 (1997): 173–178.

At Issue: Dimensions of Seriality in an Electronic World. Audiotape of presentations made at the annual meeting of the American Library Association, San Francisco, June 29, 1997. Chicago: ALA, 1997.

Barber, David. "Internet-Accessible Full-Text Electronic Journal and Periodical Collections for Libraries." *Library Technology Reports* 36, no. 5 (September/October 2000).

Barnes, John H. "One Giant Leap, One Small Step: Continuing the Migration to Electronic Journals." *Library Trends* 45, no. 3 (winter 1997): 404–415.

Boyce, Peter B. "Costs, Archiving and the Publishing Process in Electronic STM Journals." *Against the Grain* 10, no. 6 (December 1998/January 1999): 24–25.

Butler, H. Julene. "Scholarly Resources on the Internet." *Internet Research* 7, no. 1 (1997): 51–52.

Cargille, Karen, ed. "Balance Point: Lost in Cyberspace? Approaches to Subject Access to Electronic Journals." *Serials Review* 24, no. 2 (1998): 101–109.

Chadwell, Faye A. "Electronic Resources Collection Development Policy Statement Workshop: A Preconference." *Library Acquisitions: Practice and Theory* 21, no. 3 (1997): 239–240.

Chadwell, Faye A., and Sara Brownmiller. "Heads Up: Confronting the Selection and Access Issues of Electronic Journals." *Acquisitions Librarian* 11, no. 21 (1999): 21–35.

Chang, Hui-Yee, and Larry Millsap. "Cataloging Electronic Resources." *DLA Bulletin* 17, no. 1 (summer 1997): 22–24.

David, Carroll Nelson. "Problems in Defining '—Periodicals' (Electronic or Otherwise)." *Serials Review* 24, no. 2 (summer 1998): 107–109.

Davis, Trisha. "The Evolution of Selection Activities for Electronic Resources." *Library Trends* 45, no. 3 (winter 1997): 391–403.

Denning, Peter J. "The ACM Electronic Publishing Plan and Interim Copyright Policies." *Serials Librarian* 28, no. 1–2 (1996): 57–62.

Dijkstra, Joost. "Journals in Transition: From Paper to Electronic Access—the Decomate Project." *Serials Librarian* 33, no. 3–4 (1998): 243–270.

Dillon, Martin, and Erik Jul. "Cataloging Internet Resources: The Convergence of Libraries and Internet Resources." *Cataloging & Classification Quarterly* 22, no. 3–4 (1996): 197–238.

Duranceau, Ellen F., ed. "Electronic Journal Forum: Archiving and Perpetual Access for Web-based Journals; A Look at the Issues and How Five E-journal Providers Are Addressing Them." *Serials Review* 24, no. 2 (summer 1998): 110–115.

Dygert, Claire T. "New Challenges behind the Scenes: The Changing Role of the Serials Librarian in the Age of E-Publishing." *Internet Reference Services Quarterly* 3, no. 3 (1998): 7–14.

"Electronic Journal Subscriptions in Academic Libraries." *Library Systems Newsletter* 17, no. 6 (June 1997): 45–47.

Friend, Frederick J. "Inter-library Loan, Fair Dealing and the Electronic Environment." *Serials* 10, no. 3 (November 1997): 321–324.

Gadd, Elizabeth. "Copyright Clearance for the Digital Library: A Practical Guide to Gaining Electronic Permission for Journal Articles." *Serials* 10, no. 1 (March 1997): 27–32.

Gammon, Julia A. "Consortial Purchasing: The U.S. Experience with Electronic Products." *Serials* 11, no. 2 (1998): 109–114.

Garlock, Kristen L., William E. Landis, and Sherry Piontek. "Redefining Access to Scholarly Journals: A Progress Report on JSTOR." *Serials Review* 23, no. 1 (spring 1997): 1–8.

Garson, Lorrin R. "Can E-journals Save Us?—A Publisher's View." *Journal of Library Administration* 26, no. 1–2 (1998): 171–179.

Geer, Beverley, and Beatrice L. Caraway. *Notes for Serials Cataloging*, 2nd ed. Englewood, Colo.: Libraries Unlimited, 1998.

Graham, Peter S. "Requirements for the Digital Research Library." *College & Research Libraries* 56, no. 4 (July 1, 1995): 331–339.

Guernsey, Lisa. "California State University Tries to Create a New Way to Buy On-line Journals." *Chronicle of Higher Education* 45, no. 20 (January 22, 1999): A18–19.

Hannay, William M. "Legal Implications of the Digital Future." *Library Resources & Technical Services* 43, no. 4 (1999): 257–264.

Hawkins, Les. "Title Access to Full Text Journal Content Available in Aggregator Services." *Serials Review* 25, no. 4 (1999): 43–48.

Haynes, David, and David Streatfield. "Who Will Preserve Electronic Publications?" *Serials* 10, no. 3 (November 1997): 345–351.

Henderson, Tona, and Bonnie MacEwan. "Electronic Collections and Wired Faculty." *Library Trends* 45, no. 3 (winter 1997): 488–498.

Hickey, T. B. "Present and Future Capabilities of the Online Journal." *Library Trends* 43, no. 4 (spring 1995): 528–543.

Hirons, Jean, and Crystal Graham. "Issues Related to Seriality." Paper presented at the International Conference on the Principles and Future Development of AACR2, 23–25 October 1997, Toronto, Canada. Available at: http://www.nlc-bnc.ca/jsc/index.htm

Hitchcock, Steve, et al. "Towards Universal Linking for Electronic Journals." *Serials Review* 24, no. 1 (1998): 21–33.

Hobohm, Hans-Christoph. "Changing the Galaxy: On the Transformation of a Printed Journal to the Internet." *First Monday* 2, no. 11 (November 1997). Available at: http://www.firstmonday.dk.issues/issue2_11/hobohm/.

Johnson, Peggy. "Dollars and Sense: E-Resources and Collection Development and Management: Redux." *Technicalities* 20, no. 1 (January/February 2000): 1, 12–14.

Jones, Wayne, ed. *E-serials; Publishers, Libraries, Users and Standards.* New York: Haworth Press, 1998. Published simultaneously in *Serials Librarian* 33, nos. 1–2 and 3–4, 1998.

Jul, Erik. "Why Catalog Internet Resources?" *Computers in Libraries* 16, no. 1 (January 1996): 8, 10.

Ketcham, Lee, and Kathleen Born. "Projecting the Electronic Revolution while Budgeting for Status Quo." *Library Journal* 121, no. 7 (April 15, 1996): 45–51.

Ketcham-Van Orsdel, Lee, and Kathleen Born. "E-journals Come of Age: LJ's 38th Annual Periodical Price Survey." *Library Journal* 123, no. 7 (April 15, 1998): 40–45.

_____. "Pushing toward More Affordable Access: LJ's 40th Annual Periodical Price Survey." *Library Journal* 125, no. 7 (April 15, 2000): 47–52.

Kidd, Tony. "Electronic Journals: Their Introduction and Exploitation in Academic Libraries in the United Kingdom." *Serials Review* 24, no. 1 (1998): 7–14.

Kingston, Paula. "Managing the Transition from Paper to Electronic Text: Implications for Libraries and Publishers." *Serials* 10, no. 2 (July 1997): 216–223.

Kinnell, Margaret, Kate Brunskill, and Anne Morris. "Switching on Serials: The Electronic Serials in Public Libraries Project." *Serials* 11, no. 3 (November 1998): 207–214.

Krumenaker, Larry. "Stalking Serials: Full-Text Periodicals on the Web." *Searcher* 5, no. 8 (September 1997): 22–32.

Lamborn, Joan. "Virtual Trailblazing: Incorporating Electronic Journals into an Academic Library." *Serials Librarian* 31, no. 1–2 (1997): 353–359.

Larsen, Ronald L. "Directions for Defense Digital Libraries." *D-Lib Magazine* (July/August 1998). Available at: http://www.dlib.org/dlib/july98/07larsen.html

_____. "Relaxing Assumptions—Stretching the Vision: A Modest View of Some Technical Issues." *D-Lib Magazine* (April 1997). Available at: http://www.dlib.org/dlib/april97/04larsen.html

Leggate, Peter. "Acquiring Electronic Products in the Hybrid Library: Prices, Licences, Platforms and Users." *Serials* 11, no. 2 (1998): 103–108.

Leonhardt, Thomas W. "The Myth of the Electronic Library: Librarianship and Social Change in America." *Library Acquisitions: Practice and Theory* 19, no. 4 (1995): 490–493.

Lowe, Chrysanne. "A Publisher's View of E-journal Services." *Serials Review* 24, no. 1 (spring 1998): 98–99.

Luther, Judy. "Making the Most of Electronic Journals—Library and Secondary Publisher Perspectives." *Serials Librarian* 28, no. 3–4 (1996): 311–316.

_____. "Whither Electronic Journals?" *Against the Grain* 12, no. 2 (April 2000): 24, 26.

Lynch, Clifford A. "Technology and Its Implications for Serials Acquisition." *Against the Grain* 9 (February 1997): 34, 36–37.

MacEwan, Bonnie, and Mira Geffner. "The CIC Electronic Journals Collection Project." *Serials Librarian* 31, no. 1–2 (1997): 191–203.

Machovec, George S. "Electronic Journal Market Overview—1997." *Serials Review* 23, no. 2 (summer 1997): 31–44.

_____. "Key Elements in Using Technology for Library Support in Distance Education." *Online Libraries and Microcomputers* 15, no. 12 (December 1997): 1–4.

_____. "Pricing Models for Electronic Databases on the Internet." *Online Libraries and Microcomputers* 16, no. 3 (March 1998): 1–4.

_____. "User Authentication and Authorization Challenges in a Networked Library Environment." *Online Libraries and Microcomputers* 15, no. 10 (October 1997): 1–5.

Mandel, Carol A., and Robert Wolven. "Intellectual Access to Digital Documents; Joining Proven Principles with New Technologies." *Cataloging & Classification Quarterly* 22, no. 3–4 (1996): 25–42.

Martin, Lyn Elizabeth M., and Susan G. Blandy. "Guest Editorial: Embracing Change or Bracing for Change? Thinking about 'Net Serials'." *Internet Reference Services Quarterly* 3, no. 3 (1998): 1–4.

McKay, Sharon Cline. "Accessing Electronic Journals." *Database* 22, no. 2 (April/May 1999): 16, 18–23.

_____. "Partnering in a Changing Medium: The Challenges of Managing and Delivering E-journals: The Subscription Agent's Point of View." *Library Acquisitions: Practice and Theory* 22, no. 1 (1998): 23–27.

_____. "Virtual Acquisitions: Blessing or Burden." *Library Acquisitions: Practice and Theory* 21, no. 4 (1997): 495–496.

Neal, James G. "The Serials Revolution: Vision, Innovation, Tradition." *Serials Librarian* 30, no. 3–4, pt. 2 (1997): 97–105.

Nelson, Catherine. "Holdings Records for Electronic Full-Text." *DLA Bulletin* 17, no. 1 (summer 1997): 24–26.

Nilges, William. "Evolving an Integrated Electronic Journals Solution: OCLC First Search Electronic Collections Online." *Serials Librarian* 33, no. 3–4 (1998): 299–318.

O'Donnell, James. "Can E-journals Save Us? A Scholar's View." *Journal of Library Administration* 26, no.1–2 (1998): 181–186.

Ogburn, Joyce L. "Vendors and the Acquisition of Electronic Resources: Can They Help Librarians?" *Serials Review* 24, no. 1 (spring 1998): 104–106.

Risher, Carol A. "The Great Copyright Debate: Electronic Publishing Is Not Print Publishing—Vive la Difference." *Serials Librarian* 31, no. 1–2 (1997): 205–210.

Rogers, Michael. "Cal State Proposes New E-journal Buying Model." *Library Journal* 124, no. 3 (February 15, 1999): 107.

Rowley, Jennifer. "The Question of Electronic Journals." *Library Hi Tech* 18, no. 1 (2000): 46–54.

Shadle, Steven C. "A Square Peg in a Round Hole: Applying AACR2 to Electronic Journals." *Serials Librarian* 33, no. 1–2 (1998): 147–166.

_____. "Identification of Electronic Journals in the Online Catalog." *Serials Review* 24, no. 2 (summer 1998): 104–107.

Smith, Malcolm. "Hanging On to What We've Got: Economic and Management Issues in Providing Perpetual Access in an Electronic Environment." *Serials* 11, no. 2 (1998): 133–141.

Sully, Sarah E. "JSTOR: An IP Practitioner's Perspective." *D-Lib Magazine* (January 1997). Available at: http://www.dlib.org/dlib/january97/01sully.html

Tenner, Elka, and Zheng Ye (Lan) Yang. "End-user Acceptance of Electronic Journals: A Case Study from a Major Academic Research Library." *Technical Services Quarterly* 17, no. 2 (1999): 1–14.

Valauskas, Edward J. "Electronic Journals and Their Roles on the Internet." *Serials Librarian* 33, no. 1–2 (1998): 45–54.

Wakeling, Will. "Moving with the Times: E-journals in British Academic Libraries." *Serials Review* 24, no. 1 (spring 1998): 1–33.

Webb, John. "Managing Licensed Networked Electronic Resources in a University Library." *Information Technology and Libraries* 17, no. 4 (December 1998): 198–206.

White, Martin, and Peter Kibby. "Managing Electronic Serials in the Corporate Library." *Managing Information* 5, no. 8 (October 1998): 25–26, 31.

Woodward, Hazel. "Electronic Journals—The Librarian's Viewpoint." *Serials* 11, no. 3 (November 1998): 231–236.

Wordragen, Eric Jan van. "The Vendor's View of E-journal Services." *Serials Review* 24, no. 1 (spring 1998): 102–104.

CONTRIBUTORS

Pamela Bluh is the associate director for Technical Services and Administration at the Thurgood Marshall Law Library of the University of Maryland. She is a member of the American Library Association and is active in both ALCTS and LAMA. During 1996–1997, she served as chair of the ALCTS Serials Section. She is also a member of the American Association of Law Libraries. Pamela received her undergraduate degree in English from Vanderbilt University and a master's degree in German from Northwestern University. She completed her studies for the M.L.S. at Peabody College in Nashville, Tennessee. She has written and edited a number of articles and speaks occasionally at library conferences and workshops.

Faye A. Chadwell has been head of Collection Development at the University of Oregon since 1995. Before moving to the Pacific Northwest, she held positions at the University of South Carolina. Faye completed her undergraduate studies at Appalachian State University in Boone, North Carolina, and received a master's degree in English and her M.L.S. from the University of Illinois. She is active in ALA's Gay, Lesbian, Bisexual, and Transgendered Round Table and the ALCTS Collection Management and Development Section. Faye has written a number of publications and has given presentations on topics related to collection development at conferences and workshops.

Norma J. Fair is the principal cataloger at the Ellis Library, University of Missouri, Columbia, where she is responsible for the cataloging and classification of serial publications in all subjects and Roman alphabet languages. She is active in ALCTS and the Missouri Library Association.

Norma received her B.A. in English and secondary education from Sterling College and her library degree from Emporia State University. She completed a master's degree in public administration at the University of Missouri, Columbia.

Beverley Geer is the serials librarian at Questia Media in Houston, Texas. Before joining Questia Media, she was a project manager with Endeavor Information Systems and she has also held positions in several academic libraries where she was responsible for cataloging serials and monographs. In 1997 she served as president of NASIG, and she was elected chair of the ALCTS Serials Section for the 1999–2000 term. Beverley received her undergraduate degree in English and her M.L.S. from the University of Oklahoma. She is the associate editor of *Serials Review,* coeditor of the second edition of *Notes for Serials Cataloging,* and the author of numerous articles on topics ranging from series authority work to journal citation integrity. Beverley is a member of the advisory committee and a certified trainer for the Serials Cataloging Cooperative Training Program (SCCTP).

Ronald L. Larsen is currently the executive director of the Maryland Applied Information Technology Initiative (MAITI). From 1996 until 1999, Ron was the assistant director of the Information Technology Office (ITO) at the Defense Advanced Research Projects Agency (DARPA), where he developed and managed the Information Management program and the Translingual Information Detection, Extraction, and Summarization (TIDES) program. He was also responsible for DARPA's involvement in the multiagency Digital Libraries Initiative. Ron has a doctorate in computer science from the University of Maryland and has worked as a computer scientist at NASA. He is active in EDUCAUSE and the Coalition for Networked Information, and he has published numerous articles and spoken widely.

Thomas W. Leonhardt is director of the Library at the Oregon Institute of Technology in Klamath Falls, Oregon. He has over twenty-five years of experience in academic libraries, beginning at Stanford University in the mid-1970s, where he was involved with the BALLOTS project. He is a past president of the Library and Information Technology Association (LITA) and a former editor of the LITA journal, *Information Technology and Libraries.* Tom received his undergraduate degree in German and his M.L.S. from the University of California, Berkeley. He has published over fifty articles and reviews, speaks frequently at conferences and workshops, and continues to participate professionally at the national level.

George Machovec was appointed associate director of the Colorado Alliance of Research Libraries in Denver in 1999 after serving as its technical director for a number of years. Before joining the Alliance, he held several positions at Arizona State University in Tempe. George received both his undergraduate degree in physics and astronomy and his M.L.S. from the University of Arizona. He is active in ALA and serves as a member of the LITA Board of Directors. He is a member of the International Coalition of Library Consortia (ICOLC) and serves on the Regional Advisory Committee for Region 7 of the National Library of Medicine. George is the editor of the *Charleston Advisor,* which provides reviews of Web-based electronic resources, and *Online Libraries and Microcomputers.* He has written over one hundred articles, book chapters, and published conference proceedings as well as four books.

Sharon Cline McKay is a field account executive for the western United States for SilverPlatter. Before joining SilverPlatter, she represented Faxon in the same geographic region. She has worked in academic, special, and public libraries; with library automation vendors and subscription agencies; and as library school adjunct faculty. While studying full-time for her undergraduate degree in administrative studies at the University of California, Riverside, Sharon worked full-time as a library staff member. She earned her M.S.L.S. at the University of Southern California. She is active in SLA, NASIG, ALCTS, and LITA. She has written numerous articles on various aspects of serials control and is a frequent presenter at workshops and programs.

Regina Romano Reynolds is head of the National Serials Data Program at the Library of Congress. She is widely recognized for her leadership role in the development and promotion of serials standards and bibliographic control, including electronic serials and the harmonization of ISSN rules with other cataloging standards. In recognition of her many outstanding contributions to the field of serials librarianship, Regina was presented with the Bowker/Ulrich's Serials Librarianship Award by the ALCTS Serials Section in 1999. Regina is well known as an enthusiastic presenter at national and international conferences and as the author of numerous articles and reports. She received her M.L.S. from the University of Michigan.

Steven C. Shadle has been the serials cataloger at the University of Washington Libraries since 1995. He is responsible for the original and complex copy cataloging of serials in all subject areas and all formats. He also works for OCLC/WLN's Techpro program, providing original cataloging for Idaho State government publications held by the Idaho State Library. Steve has considerable experience as a lecturer, most recently at the School of Library and Information Science at the University of Washington. He has an undergraduate degree in linguistics and received his M.L.S. from the University of Washington. Steve did postgraduate work at SUNY Albany in the application of new technologies to the organization of materials. He has published several articles and made a number of presentations dealing with the application of cataloging rules to electronic serials.

Sarah E. Sully has been a member of the Technology Transactions Group at Morrison & Foerster LLP in New York City since the spring of 1999. Her areas of specialization include intellectual property and matters of copyright and trademark law, particularly as they relate to Internet law. Before joining Morrison & Foerster, Sarah was general counsel and director of Publisher Relations at JSTOR. In that capacity, she was responsible for conducting negotiations and arranging the licensing of many of the journals that comprise the JSTOR database. She did her undergraduate work at Dartmouth College and received her J.D. cum laude from the Benjamin N. Cardozo School of Law. Sarah has written numerous articles on copyright law. She is a member of the Copyright Society of the U.S.A. and chairs the steering committee of the Friends of Active Copyright Education (FA©E) initiative.

Raye Lynn Thomas has been an associate librarian and reference coordinator at the Ruben Salazar Library at Sonoma State University since 1994. Her responsibilities include reference desk operations and document delivery services, and she also provides connectivity advice and reference assistance to on-site and distance education students. Raye Lynn has a B.A. in art history from San Francisco State University, and she received her M.L.I.S. from the University of California, Berkeley. She is active professionally at both the state and national levels. Raye Lynn serves on the California State University Electronic Access to Information Resources Committee, which evaluates electronic resources for consortial acquisition. She is also active in ALA's International Relations Round Table. Raye Lynn has taught library research courses at Sonoma State and at San Francisco State Universities.

Dan Tonkery was appointed president of Faxon, Rowecom's Academic and Medical Services in March 2000. Dan has over thirty years of experience both as a librarian and as a vendor. He received his M.L.S. from the University of Illinois and began his professional career at the National

Library of Medicine. He later became Associate University Librarian for Technical Services at UCLA, where he was instrumental in the development of the ORION integrated library system. Before becoming president of Faxon, Dan held senior management positions with several subscription agencies, including Faxon, Readmore, and Dawson. He has been an active member of NASIG since its inception and was elected NASIG president for 2000. He is also a member of the board of the Council on Library and Information Resources.

Friedemann A. Weigel is a managing partner and director of Information Systems for Harrassowitz, the internationally known bookseller and subscription agent. Friedemann is active in a number of standard-setting organizations, including the International Committee for EDI for Serials (ICEDIS) and the Serials Industry Systems Advisory Committee (SISAC). He was elected chairman of the Pan-European Book Sector EDI Group, known as EDItEUR, for the year 2000. Before joining the management team at Harrassowitz, Friedemann completed his studies in business at the University of Hamburg. He is extremely knowledgeable about serials industry standards and speaks frequently in the United States and in Europe on topics ranging from EDI to managing electronic resources.

INDEX